Making Schooling Relevant for the Global Age

Fulfilling Our Moral Obligation

R. D. Nordgren

SCARECROWEDUCATION
Lanham, Maryland • Toronto • Oxford
2003

Published in the United States of America
by ScarecrowEducation
An imprint of The Rowman & Littlefield Publishing Group, Inc.
4501 Forbes Boulevard, Suite 200, Lanham, Maryland 20706
www.scarecroweducation.com

PO Box 317
Oxford
OX2 9RU, UK

British Library Cataloguing in Publication Information Available

Library of Congress Cataloging-in-Publication Data

Nordgren, R. D., 1960–
    Making schooling relevant for the global age : fulfilling our moral
obligation / R.D. Nordgren.
        p.   cm.
    Includes bibliographical references and index.
    ISBN 1-57886-025-3 (pbk. : alk. paper)
    1. Education–Aims and objectives–United States.   2. Public
schools–United States.   3. Educational change–United States.
I. Title.
LA217.2 .N67   2003
370'.973–dc21   2003011919

∞ ™ The paper used in this publication meets the minimum
requirements of American National Standard for Information
Sciences—Permanence of Paper for Printed Library Materials,
ANSI/NISO Z39.48-1992. Manufactured in the United States of
America.

CONTENTS

Introduction   1
  Connecting with the Swedes   7
  Is Trust the Key?   10
  Defending the Swedes   14
  Educators' Efficacy: What We Can Do in the Schools   18

Part I: Failing to Catch the Next Wave of Civilization

Chapter 1   Accountability in U.S. Schools   23
               What Accountability Really Does to Schools   27
               Punishing for Success?   33

Chapter 2   Waves of Civilization   37
               Stuck in the Past   37
               Class Warfare   40
               Making Sense of the Third Wave   42

Chapter 3   Those Who Control Schooling   47

Part II: Major Obstacles to Change

Chapter 4   Power and Control   59
               Control in U.S. Schools   61
               School Structure and Control   64
               Fear and the Overemphasis on Control   70

Chapter 5   Balancing Collectivism and Individualism   75
               Trust, Individualism, and Hero Worship   76
               All for One, One for All   82
               Japan and the Rise of a Collectivist Economy   84
               African American Collectivism and Social Justice   86
               Forcing Industrial-Age Schooling onto African
               Americans   88

Selling Collectivism to Those in Power 91
Establishing Collectivism as an Attainable Goal 92

Part III: A New Model of Schooling for the Global Age and Beyond

Chapter 6   A New Model for a New Era 97
The Need for Core Values 101
A Global-Age Model for Schooling 106
Roles of Stakeholders 113
Goals of Global-Age Schools 128

Chapter 7   Vision for Global-Age Schooling 133
An Educational Philosophy to Embrace 133
Autonomy of Students and Teachers 137
Moving Carefully toward Responsibility 141
Changing Roles within the Schools 143
Responsibility and Internalized Motivation 146
Creating and Sustaining the Essential Value: Trust 149
Communities of Learning: Building Trust 152
Individualized Learning 159
Considering Personality Types for Leadership and
    Change 163
Starting Early 170

Chapter 8   Change and Schooling 175
Shifting, Pragmatic Knowledge 178
Promoting and Facilitating Change 180

Chapter 9   Our Moral Obligation 187
Social Justice and Democracy 187

Appendix A   Swedish National Curriculum for the Compulsory
School, the Pre-School Class, and the Leisure-
Time Centre (LPO 94) 193

Appendix B   Swedish National Curriculum for the Pre-School 199

References 203

Index 207

About the Author 211

INTRODUCTION

A culture of distrust has developed in our public schools and within the communities that our schools serve. This distrust, fueled by politicians and the media, developed from schools' refusal to change from indus-trial-age institutions to those that serve the needs of a global-age society. A result of this distrust is the accountability and standards movements that seek to send U.S. schooling further back into a time that no longer exists in this nation. Furthermore, these movements threaten to broaden and deepen the chasm between the haves and have-nots in our society. By adopting a new model of schooling, our schools can not only halt the irrelevant and dangerous "standardization of schooling" but can regain the trust of the public. The general public, however, along with most politicians, media, and educators, do not comprehend the need for schools to "globalize"; they seem to know that something is amiss, yet cannot correctly identify the problem. Instead, they simply do more of the same: more tests for students as well as for teachers and administra-tors.

It must be understood that success in global-age schools cannot be measured by standardized tests; success will be realized only when stu-dents become fully active participants in democracies and effective workers in global-age organizations. Change is painful. Those who hold power in our society might not immediately enjoy the results of the dis-empowered gaining the insight and the strategies necessary to become part of the democratic process, but all of us will reap the benefits of a populace that is truly educated and responsible for its own actions. In-deed, the health of our nation depends on the acceptance of a new model of schooling.

In this book, I hope to convey to the reader the desperate dilemma in which our schools currently find themselves. There is a new model for schooling, one that allows our citizens to establish a real democracy

1

as well as global-age organizations that will become the standard for the rest of the world. Although I repeatedly warn the reader about the obstacles that must be overcome to establish such a schooling system, I firmly believe that we Americans can succeed in accomplishing this daunting task. As I call for comprehensive change in our system of schooling, the reader will be able to envision the results this will have on our society. Schooling can and should be a catalyst for necessary change in all aspects of society. It is our moral obligation to ensure that schooling is relevant for a new "wave of civilization," one for which we are currently unprepared and, frighteningly, an era whose existence we reject. The current ill-fated and dangerously reactionary school reform efforts seek to take our society backward to a day that no longer exists or, more likely, never existed.

After a school board meeting I attended a few years ago, some teachers and principals held four forty-five-minute seminars. At one of the seminars titled "Schools for Tomorrow, Today," an elementary school principal was the only presenter. An assortment of parents, teachers, and interested community members (about thirty in all) took the seats closest to the presenter. The principal opened by saying that the school experiences that everyone in the room had were irrelevant to what was happening in her school and the other schools in her small district. Those in attendance, she went on, had been educated for the industrial age. Her district's schools, she boldly stated, were preparing their children for the global age. This school board meeting was in Sweden and the principal's district was indeed focused on preparing its students for the postindustrial age.

The room was silent after the principal made her statement, yet I saw no angry faces nor did I sense any disagreement from the audience. The principal was to be commended for her courage in saying this to the parents, teachers, and community members in the audience. In my view, she and her school district were indeed intent on making schooling relevant in a global economy and in a world with blurred national boundaries due to the world's economy and the transience of its workforce. This principal's courage gave me the resolve to speak out for schooling in America that was relevant for the global age. I had for years believed that our nation's schools were being left behind in an age that had passed, but in this age of school accountability, I was afraid to openly express my beliefs because those who control U.S. schooling are not only determined to bury schooling deeper into the industrial age but also to bury those who oppose them. U.S. educators and those who influence schooling are ignorant of or unwilling to change to meet the challenges of a new wave of civilization (a phrase I borrow from Alvin Toffler's *The Third Wave* [1980]). In this book, I describe both the need for a new model of schooling and the model itself, a model that allows our citizens to be prepared to survive and thrive in the global economy as well as to become active and participating members of our democracy—a system of government deeply wounded by widespread apathy.

I share with the readers my experiences in Sweden in hopes that the Swedish schools can be an inspiration for us. Throughout the book, my references to Sweden are an attempt to demonstrate a system where learning takes precedence over the control of students; where socialization is favored over academics (yet international studies find Swedish high school students to be superior to Americans in math and science [NCES 1999]). Scholars from all over the world, including the United States, developed most of the strategies employed by the Swedes to create their effective system of schooling. We Americans have neglected to implement these strategies and are suffering from the consequences as our students and our society are in great danger of being left behind in the global age. placing on personal success

The creation of a system of relevant and effective schooling will allow all Americans to be prepared to live and work in this postindustrial society. At present, a great number of our people, probably the vast majority, are not prepared for success in this new era. Effective education economically and politically empowers all people of a nation. Military might alone does not ensure a successful, enduring nation-state or society; we must therefore strive to reduce the strain caused by growing social and economic depravity. We only need to examine the failure of the former Soviet Union as evidence. A new model of schooling, one that empowers every citizen, must be designed and implemented before more of our children are left behind in the age of globalization. Although educators must take the lead in this design and implementation, they will need the support of those who hold power in our democracy: politicians and the business community. It will take nothing less than a combined effort of all U.S. schooling's stakeholders to ensure success.

Certain traits or qualities will be desired of both citizens and workers for this new global age. Sweden has established school systems that reflect what research in economics, sociology, and education suggest are effective in our postindustrial world. The most startling aspect of the Swedish school system may be the promoting of social skills over academics, especially at an early age. I refer to this and other findings from my experiences with Swedish schools (as well as American schools) as evidence that a new vision of schooling can be developed, despite both nations' recent social and economic challenges.

The title *Making Schooling Relevant for the Global Age* implies that our system of schooling is not designed for the global era, which is apparent to anyone who carefully examines its structure, its curricula, and the inequities of its funding. It is, in fact, an industrial-age relic. My intent is to express to educators and noneducators alike that our system is not conducive to fostering global citizens and workers. But so as not to simply be another critic of education with no effective solution (and there are many), I describe a model of schooling based on core values essential for the global age—a model that is accompanied by new roles for all school stakeholders. I also offer a way of structuring existing schools so that they more resemble the global-age organizations that have proven to be successful. Essentially, I describe a whole new way of schooling in America, a new model that is desperately needed. The model I promote might seem somewhat vague to the reader. It is vague by design so that it can be shaped to meet the needs of each state, district, and distinct school community. The last thing that U.S. education needs is another critic; the next to last thing it needs is another idiotic, ironclad remedy to resolve its complex problems. This new model of schooling is a "one size fits all" approach in that it advocates fluid organizations that can constantly change to meet the needs of those who are directly and indirectly affected by schooling.

As I criticize our current system of schooling, I want to assure the reader that our schools have never been more successful at accomplishing the goal that they are structured and funded to achieve: providing as many students as possible with a rudimentary education, one that will allow them to be able to work in a menial job and socialize with those of similar economic, class, racial, and religious backgrounds. This is essentially what twentieth-century compulsory schooling was devised to do. It produced a factory-ready worker as well as a citizen who could live within a racially and socially segregated society. But this is morally wrong. The percentage of the American workforce in factories has been in decline for decades, replaced by a highly volatile service and techno-logical economy that requires a different type of worker. With this new economy, it is our moral obligation to allow for *all* to have equal footing in our society, both in the economic and the political sense. This, I argue, is crucial because globalization causes nations' boundaries and political alliances to continuously shift, thus requiring industry as well as its citizenry to take a holistic view of the world instead of one that is inwardly focused, ignoring the rest of the global village.

To promote my stance that America's schools are failing to meet the needs of a new global age, I describe just how schools arrived at where they are today: industrial-age relics that are the targets of criticism from both the right and left ends of the political spectrum. It is also a system that is highly supervised and controlled by lay people (noneducators) under the guise of the accountability movement and the subsequently imposed standards movement, with its constant testing of students and teachers and teacher-proof curricula. I contend that these movements impede schools' development into global-age organizations, and are used by school reformers to move schooling backward, deeper into the now-defunct industrial age. I compare the current goals of our system of schooling to what scholars from various fields say we should know and be like in the global age. I briefly explain the three waves of civiliza-tion as described by Toffler, and U.S. education's reluctance to meet the needs of the third wave, globalization. I then ask the reader to examine who controls schooling and what their intentions are.

In order to meet the needs of the global village, U.S. schooling must thoroughly change its structure, that is, it must "restructure." In studies of organizations, restructuring signifies not only a complete change of order but also a shift in the way people in the organization think—a "paradigm shift," if I may use what is already a tired, and worn-out ex-pression. Restructuring differs drastically from reform in that the latter is merely making adjustments to the overall organizational structure; that is what schooling has been doing for decades, especially since the publication of *A Nation at Risk* in 1983 (National Commission on Excellence in Education). These reforms have not led to forward change, only "more of the same": more testing, more high school credits, more school hours, more standards.

An analogy to restructuring schooling is a huge national net surrounding all our schools. This net would allow all 40,000 public schools to have a unified purpose while also allowing this purpose to filter its way out into society. Instead of schools being a mirror of society, perhaps they can become the lens through which we view a new vision of ourselves as a nation and as people living in a global village.

The purpose of schooling must be to foster a democracy that empowers people of all races, religions, cultures, and socioeconomic backgrounds (or SES, as used by educators to denote the educational level and income of a child's parents or guardians) so that they can and will allow democracy to proliferate while participating and directing the course of the global economy. This endeavor requires not only the political and moral support of the American people but also that those who lead this changing education system be the presumed educational professionals, meaning our "educators." By the term *educator*, I include teachers, school and district administrators, and colleges of education professors. I in no way intend to keep parents and the community out of the decision making. They, along with the students, are schooling's clients. The larger curricula, which would be value laden (as are the Swedish curricula), should be written by a consortium of national leaders with representatives from all sectors of society, not simply politicians, selected business executives, and token educators, as have been the reforms of the past two decades. This consortium would include experts from all fields and industry, but should especially include visionaries whose input should prove invaluable.

For too long, education has had no vision; it has simply reacted to society. In the past few decades, education has not even reacted. It is, however, the educators who are the crucial element of any decision-making group concerning education's future. The implementation of a new schooling model must be enacted at the professional discretion of the educator. The most important value of the curricula would be a democracy that is empowering; students would by design be involved with the decision making at the local level in the development and implementation. Although this application of a new schooling model would begin at the local level, national controls are necessary to ensure equity. I am not advocating a laissez-faire approach to supervision of schooling but instead one that is built around trust. As a Swedish principal reminded me, democracy depends on trusting the people, and its continuance depends on people taking the responsibility that is expected with that trust.

From my experiences in American and Swedish schools as well as what is advocated in the prevailing globalization literature, I offer some ways in which our schools and school systems can better prepare our children for the third wave of civilization. First is the establishment of learning communities within school organizations, creating caring, nurturing environments that are superior to traditional school models. Next, power must be shared within the classroom, the school, and the entire school system. With this sharing of power must come a transference of control for learning, a transference from adults in authority positions (teachers, administrators) to the learners. Fostering collaboration in the school setting allows not only for students to be prepared to work in the global economy but also to become more socially conscious—that is, better global citizens. Change disturbs most of us because we are essentially "creatures of habit," but change is essential and can be accomplished if designed and promoted to our various populations and personalities. Without the support of the vast majority of our school personnel and the general society, especially those who control schooling's destiny, we cannot expect change to occur—at least, not progressive change. Finally, I question the reasons for compulsory education, helping the reader understand what it is I am promoting: the fostering of the global citizen/worker who actively participates in the global economy as well as the worldwide network of societies known as the global village.

As mentioned previously, the Swedes have taken many progressive ideas and have implemented them nationwide. Although Sweden's population is quite small (about the size of New Jersey), this nationwide implementation was still quite an accomplishment. To advance a national plan in the United States will be much more daunting.

CONNECTING WITH THE SWEDES

In 1999, a Swedish principal and a former superintendent visited the large middle/high school in Florida where I was an assistant principal.

The two Swedes were part of a contingent of approximately forty Swedish educators who visited a dozen or so schools in the Tampa Bay area. I took great pains to ensure that my Swedish visitors would see all of my school of 3,600 students, both what made us proud and what needed our attention, and not simply to take the "wet paint" tour. I drove them to and from my school both days, about a two-hour round trip from their Tampa motel, during which time we engaged in insightful yet often unsettling conversation about American education. On the second morning's drive to school, I was describing my district's embracing of site-based management, where more and more of our school's decisions were made at the school level instead of at the central office.

I must have seemed to be bragging about our progressive philosophy, as the former superintendent asked me what percentage of the school's actual budget was controlled by the principal and her staff. I knew she had me. Smiling, I said "no more than about 10 percent," because I knew salaries account for about 85 percent of a school's budget. She said that in Sweden, the schools are typically given the power to control salaries. I was impressed by this example of power sharing between school and school district, and I was to be impressed further as I delved deeper into my study of education in Sweden. As an assistant principal, I could not imagine being trusted with the power to decide how much compensation a teacher could receive. What criteria did the Swedes use to determine this? What effect did this have on teachers' morale? I wanted to find out more.

After two days of visiting elementary, middle, high, and adult/technical schools in five school districts, the Swedes met in Tampa to report their findings of American schools—or at least, Tampa-area schools. The Swedes, in their modest and subtle way, startled their American hosts by describing our schools and those in them as being infatuated with control. Teachers controlled students, principals controlled teachers and students, central office administrators controlled everyone at the schools, and the state government controlled the school districts. (Since that time, the federal government has also been doing its best to mandate its will upon schooling at all levels through the No Child Left Behind Act of 2001.) This is what the Swedes surmised from only two days of visits and three days of discussions with American principals and teachers.

From my graduate studies on school organizations, including business management, I knew the Swedes were right. It hurt to hear this from outsiders, but their remarks were valid. Many of my colleagues were dismayed by the reports. Perhaps they could not comprehend another way of schooling other than what we were doing in Florida or, for that matter, the entire United States, as the Florida model based on the infamous Florida "A+ Plan" of using testing to bribe and control schools and school districts appears to be the model of choice for all states and is highly touted by federal politicians. What gave the Swedes the right to criticize us? I imagined my fellow administrators as thinking, We are, after all, the most powerful nation on Earth. The Swedes were citizens of a tiny, insignificant nation (at least to us ethnocentric Americans) of fewer than 9 million people. Our state of Florida had nearly twice as many people. We would soon discover for ourselves what gave the Swedes the right to criticize our schools: their schools, in comparison with ours, were greatly "evolved" toward the goal of making them relevant in the global age.

Later that year, many of the principals and teachers of the schools visited by the Swedes in April accepted the opportunity to visit schools in Sweden. I trekked to a high school in northern Sweden, the school where my visiting Swedish principal worked. I spent two days at my Swedish friend's school of 2,000 sixteen- to nineteen-year-old students. I was astounded by what I saw. Imagine a classroom where the students continuously engage in collaborative learning; the teacher acts as facilitator, collaborating as adviser and/or mentor; students come and go out of the classroom without teacher permission or even acknowledgment; the teacher neither gives, nor seemingly needs to give, directives in learning or in discipline. Now I ask the reader to remember the numerous classrooms from his or her past (and, perhaps, present) where students work on mundane assignments; where the teacher's main role is that of disciplinarian, sitting at his or her desk, giving students "the look" if they fall off task and dare to disturb his or her own task of grading papers in silence (or reading the newspaper!). Although I have occasionally experienced the type of schooling I found in Sweden both as an observer and as a classroom teacher, I have more often experienced the second scenario as a student in American schools. The first scenario, where students are actively engaged in meaningful learning, best prepares them for the global age. The second classroom prepares them for the factories of the industrial age, an age that has long since passed in the United States and in the other "globalized" nations.

After our visit, we met with the thirty or so American educators who had observed schools in other parts of Sweden. We were to report our findings to the Swedes. Instead of reporting in groups for each level of school observed, as did the Swedes in Tampa, we reported as a panel of individuals. Each of us gave a brief synopsis of our observations and our opinions of what we had experienced. Although few of us collaborated in preparing our reports, each of the reports was consistent: the overarching theme was that of trust. This contrasted greatly with the Swedes' description of control in our Florida schools. Teachers trusted students, principals trusted teachers and students, central offices trusted schools, and I would surmise from later investigation, the national government trusted the communities to do what was best to educate children. Our American egos were deflated. The people from this relatively tiny nation seemed to have taken all of the progressive education movement's "best practices" and broadly implemented them. I, for one, wanted to find out how they accomplished this, knowing that we in America were experiencing wave after wave of "reforms," rendering our schools into irrelevant, industrial-age relics that were further widening the already gaping chasm between the social classes as well as races.

IS TRUST THE KEY?

Believing trust to be the driving force behind the Swedes' success in implementing progressive school restructuring, I examined the prevailing literature on trust, especially trust in organizations. In developing a case study of two high schools, one in central Sweden and the school in northern Sweden that I had visited in 1999, I was determined to find out how the Swedes built such trusting learning environments. In 2000, while interviewing one of the principals (there were two) in the school in central Sweden, I was asked why my questions focused on trust and not responsibility. Furthermore, the principal inquired, why not democracy? I immediately understood the relationship between trust and responsibility, as the literature on trust was consistent in its acknowledgment of the unwavering connection between trust and responsibility. If management, which includes teachers for students and principals for teacher, is to demonstrate trust through allowing more decision making to be made by others and granting more autonomy to them, then it must expect and receive responsible action from the employees. Without this responsibility, trust would immediately dissolve.

When American schools attempt to implement site-based management—and I acknowledge both the flaws and successes in these implementations—they often find that the teachers do not take on responsibility when trusted to make decisions. Their lack of responsibility amounted to not caring enough to participate in the decision-making process, or so it seemed. Of course, these teachers were usually not given the training to make good decisions or any decisions at all, nor did they trust administrators to believe that their decisions would be implemented. What I did not comprehend from my discussion with the Swedish principal was the notion of democracy. I asked her, "Why democracy?" She then described the role the three values (democracy, trust, and responsibility) played in the two Swedish national curricula.

National curricula? I did not like the sound of that. I envisioned an uncaring, powerful national bureaucracy dictating what students should learn and how teachers should teach, much like most American states' departments of education attempt to do. The principal briefly described the curricula, one for the compulsory schooling of seven- to fifteen-year-olds and the other for noncompulsory high schools and adult schools. Her description was that of values-laden documents that emphasized the fostering of responsibility in students through trusting, democratic learning environments. Instantly, my focus on trust expanded to include two other foci: responsibility and democracy in the schools.

I returned to Sweden the following year, this time with a study that focused on one community, the one in central Sweden where the insightful principal worked. This new study examined how trust, student responsibility, and democracy through shared power were supported in a feeder system of schools: an elementary, middle, and high school where about 75 percent of the students in the high school had attended both the middle and the elementary schools. I came to Sweden with a rudimentary understanding of the simple yet remarkable document called the Swedish National Curriculum; I found there to be three, instead of the two previously mentioned. There are curricula for the compulsory and the secondary/adult levels; yet another curriculum had just been introduced for the noncompulsory preschool level. These three provide the all-important basis of the Swedish model of schooling. All three curricula are essentially the same in that they are value laden. I intended to discover if the Swedish schools I studied supported trust, responsibility, and shared power as described in the curricula.

The first sign of trust in this study was when the principals allowed me to visit any classroom I wanted, at any time. A basic schedule for observations was devised at each school, yet I was free to come and go as I pleased and took advantage of this carte blanche opportunity. Students were curious about my comings and goings, as would be expected, but because of the nature of the teaching methods used, I was not an interruption. Many teachers whose classrooms I observed did not seem to know that I was from the United States and was conducting a study, nor did they seem to mind my presence. They and their students simply went about their business of learning.

What I found in the schools was quite remarkable. Students in all schools developed their own learning plans, beginning with preschool children (four- to six-year-olds). Although the youngest students did not have their learning plans in written form, the evidence suggested that they were deeply involved with the development of these plans. Preschool children would sit in circles on Monday mornings to decide what they were to do during the week, the teacher acting as facilitator. On Fridays, they discussed their learning for the week and then completed a self-assessment consisting of smiling or frowning faces for each activity conducted, followed by more discussion. This was the beginning of their democratic schooling experiences.

In the high school, students agreed that they had a great amount of input regarding their learning, but insisted that they should have more. Indeed, they seemed to hunger for more power. They had four years in which they were to reach the standards developed through the national department of education (Skolverket) for all sixteen high school–level programs offered in each of the Swedish communities. The standards were found to be scant and somewhat vague in comparison to American state standards, and most interesting, the means to these ends were decided by negotiations between the students and the teachers, not high-stakes testing.

Teachers in the high school and, for that matter, in the middle school, were difficult to identify when I first entered the rooms. They dressed casually and rarely began their class by standing in front of the room and addressing the students. Instead, students came into the rooms in an easygoing manner (there were no bells), began working on a project, and the teachers would sit next to them, working individually with each student or, more likely, engaged with a group of students. Oddly, all teachers were addressed by their first name only, a practice I had previously witnessed in other parts of Sweden. (In contrast, I have never been to an American public school where the roles of the students and teachers were not made distinct by the use of "Mister," "Mrs.," or "Miss"; very few female teachers prefer "Ms." I cannot help but think that the use of these titles only interferes with the all-important connections between students and teachers.)

Elementary school children played outdoors on an icy hill and on a skating rink between and during classes. Usually a teacher was around, but sometimes not. At another school not in the study, I participated in a mid-morning "tea" given by two eleven-year-olds for all the adults at the school. When I asked where the other 200 students were, a teacher pointed out the window to where they were sledding and skating on a frozen pond. To my amazement, no adults were outside to supervise. I asked what would happen if a child were to get hurt. "Oh, another child would let us know, I suppose," was the answer from the principal. Apparently, Sweden was not a very litigious society and, it seemed, a trusting one. In American schools, it is of the utmost importance that all children be supervised at all times. This need for supervision, unfortunately, supercedes any need for student learning or responsibility for one's self.

In addition to the students' writing their own learning plans, the lunchrooms were excellent examples of how responsible students can be, if given the chance. At all three schools, students ate and socialized without formal adult supervision. The elementary school teachers ate with their students in a small cafeteria, but gave no directives to the children. Again, I found myself amazed, this time at the sight of seven- and eight-year-old children eating with real knives, forks, and spoons as well as glass cups. No plastic "sporks" nor disposable plates and other eating utensils as are found in the United States. Children demonstrated mature, responsible table manners, even bussing their tables when finished and recycling what could be recycled. The same scenario was found in the middle school. At the high school, adults ate separately in a small room, leaving the students adult-free except for the lunchroom servers (although I observed in another high school in Sweden the general public coming in to eat with the students). No adults or students could recall a problem stemming from this lack of adult supervision.

At the middle and high schools, students were found in snack rooms and recreation areas, again with little or no adult supervision. In fact, the only adults consistently in the vicinity were those who worked the snack counter. The middle school students had sofas and music in one snack room, and volleyball, table tennis, billiards, and other games in the second snack room. Adults insisted that no problems ever arose from students misbehaving in these rooms.

As an American teacher and administrator, this lack of control in and out of the classroom was quite startling. "What happens when students do not do what they are supposed to do?" I asked teachers on several occasions. I would receive a puzzled look and sometimes a reply of "Why wouldn't they?" I must clarify that the students were not merely demonstrating blind obedience (a characteristic detrimental for a society that desires to have a true democracy), because there were no directives from teachers or other adults "to do" or "not to do" something. They simply went about their business of learning. Elementary teachers told me that they concentrated on social skills rather than academics in the early years yet international studies suggest that by high school, Swedes outperform students from many industrialized nations, including the United States. One Swedish teacher told me that their first intention is for the children to learn to socialize well with others. "What good is it to teach them to read and write if they are only going to end up in prison?" she asked. Point well taken.

DEFENDING THE SWEDES

When discussing the findings from my studies of Swedish schools with other American educators, I am invariably told that I was studying a homogeneous population where one culture is shared. On the contrary, some of the schools I observed in the community in which the study occurred had student populations where as many as 85 percent were immigrants or sons and daughters of immigrants. These immigrants generally were not from other Scandinavian or Western European nations, but came mostly from Vietnam, Kurdistan, Somalia, and China. The students came to school speaking many other languages and not well versed in the nuances of the Swedish culture, yet somehow they took on the responsibility of learning and of getting along with others. If the emphasis on socialization, especially in the early grades, worked in this environment, it would be logical to assume that it would succeed in the multicultural schools in the United States as well.

In addition to the social dimensions of democracy, trust, and responsibility, I was interested to know if Swedish schools were preparing their students for the global economy. It was nice that they all seemed to get along and quite beneficial, if not crucial, that they seemed ready to participate in the democracies of the global village. But were these students gaining the skills and knowledge necessary for them to succeed in the ever-changing world of globalization? Studying the prevalent literature on workforce skills, including the SCANS report (a 1992 U.S. Department of Labor report that sought to describe what students should know, do, and be like in the economy of the twenty-first century), I extrapolated from this literature on workforce skills the four dimensions of teamwork, pragmatic technical skills, problem solving, and entrepreneurship. Indeed, the lower levels of schooling concentrated on social skills, yet the Swedish high schools were determined to prepare students for the global workforce as well as the global village.

As mentioned earlier, each community must offer all sixteen of the career-centered programs of study. These programs at my most recent study's high school were treated as schools within schools in that teachers typically worked in only one program and were given significant autonomy within that program. The Skolverket set the guidelines for the programs but these were rather flexible, allowing for the students and teachers to decide among themselves what would be learned. The three main subject areas (Swedish, English, and math) existed in each program, but these subjects were learned through the lens of the specific career area of the program. Two programs did not appear to be career oriented but were more college preparatory. When mentioning this to Swedish teachers, they were quick to point out that students in every program could, in theory, be accepted into a university (university admission in Sweden is quite competitive, with only about one in three students gaining admission). Nonetheless, I would venture to say that those students in the college-preparatory programs would have an advantage over other students in passing each university's admissions criteria.

In the eleven programs offered at the high school in the study, the four dimensions of workforce skills and competencies were supported. High school students, as did students of all ages, worked collaboratively. The few who worked individually did so at their own request but this, they said, was only temporary. Marketable technical skills were to be gained in the various programs, and problem solving was inherent in the project-based curricula developed by the students with the help of the teachers.

One focus of the Swedes' visit to Tampa Bay schools in 1999 was to determine how American schools encouraged entrepreneurship in their students. The Skolverket desired the fostering of this "American" trait in the Swedish schools because the European Union was growing in size and stature and the Swedes wanted to ensure that their brightest pupils and the jobs they might create would stay in Sweden. What they found in Florida schools, of course, was the insidious stifling of the hallmarks of entrepreneurship: risk taking and creativity. Florida schools, as do most all public schools in the United States, are bent on controlling teachers, students, and curricula. I naively assumed that if the Swedes were looking to the United States to help increase entrepreneurship in their schools, then risk taking and creativity must be almost nonexistent in Swedish education. But creativity abounded in all the schools in the study. By the instructional methods used and the structures of the schools, creativity was a natural by-product, as was risk taking. Developing their own learning requires students to be both creative and risk takers. Two programs that I observed in the high school actually had classes in entrepreneurship, where students were allotted money to open businesses in the community. It was rare that these businesses lost money, according to the teachers.

Of course, schools like the ones I studied in Sweden exist in other parts of the world, including the United States. Yet from my visits and my colleagues' visits to schools in Sweden, these "constructivist" learning environments (where students are allowed to create knowledge from their own experiences and, thus, allowed substantial autonomy) appeared to be nationwide. According to some Swedish teachers, only ten years prior to my last study, their schools had resembled the United States in their British-style approach to education, where teachers were to simply "pour" information into the students' open minds. How could this transformation be accomplished so quickly? As one Swedish principal said, "It was painful." Asking teachers and administrators to share power with children, profoundly changing the roles they played in schools, must have indeed been painful, but it appeared to be working. One veteran teacher said that he had had his doubts about the new system when it was enacted following the 1994 Education Reform Act, but he could now see that his students were much more prepared to live and work in a democracy. (This term was used often in my conversations with Swedish teachers and principals.) The structure of each school's management and the instructional methods used promoted the skills deemed necessary to succeed in the global economy. Yet, could this be replicated in the United States?

First, I need to explain that the Swedes do not encounter the one consistent indicator of school success (or should I say lack of success?): poverty. The social democracy that prevails in Sweden does not allow for great socioeconomic differences (Johnson and Gahler 1997). In fact, I could not tell the difference between a student of unemployed parents and a student whose parents were professionals. The differences in income between someone working the counter at McDonald's and a medical doctor are not nearly as significant as they would be in America. The social net provided by the state allows the unemployed to live in relative comfort—relative, that is, to how those in the United States must live.

Even subtracting the element of poverty, I believe Americans cannot develop and sustain this Swedish style of schooling without structuring the schools and school systems in such a way that power is shared. The bureaucratic organizations that exist at the state and local levels would have to give way to flatter, more responsive systems. With the implementation of state and national standards in recent years, the U.S.

school bureaucracies have grown, further removing the clients of education from true decision making; ironically, this growth in bureaucracy is contrary to the conservative philosophy that now controls school reform. The Swedes have national curricula for three different levels of schools, but these curricula are malleable at the local and even the classroom levels. Local control was, in fact, a primary initiative of the 1994 reform.

School reform in the United States, especially since the publication of *A Nation at Risk* in 1983, is to essentially "do more of the same." I must agree with Gerald Bracey, the eminent education statistician, that schools are doing a better job at what they have been asked to do than ever before: to educate as many children as possible in the most efficient manner. The concern is the term "educate." Is education merely a regurgitation of often useless facts (the ability to perform well on standardized tests)? Or is it the gaining of skills necessary to flourish in the future? Alvin Toffler noted over thirty years ago in his famous work *Future Shock* (1970) that schools prepare students to (1) be on time, (2) be obedient, and (3) perform repetitive tasks. These are the skills required for success in the industrial age—but the industrial age has long since passed in the United States. Why should we continue to support an education system that prepares citizens to live in the past?

EDUCATORS' EFFICACY: WHAT WE CAN DO IN THE SCHOOLS

Keeping in mind what I experienced in Sweden, and what the Swedes observed in Florida, we have to ask ourselves: What can educators do to develop schools that enable students to be prepared for the global age? I firmly believe that politicians cannot be counted on to lead the way because they are compelled to control and punish failing schools, fed by the media with their insatiable appetites for headlines. Besides, much of K–12 schooling's problems would be eliminated if politicians faced up to their obligation of eradicating poverty. Instead, they turn their backs to what I believe to be the defining problem of this new century, dumping the task of alleviating poverty onto the schools—thus, diverting attention away from their callous disregard of the poor, who are often people of color. Yes, Lyndon Johnson's War on Poverty made significant gains, but this war has been lost due to blatant disregard of the poor in the past few decades and the underclass's failure to gain political clout.

Schools can indeed do much to help alleviate poverty, but not by themselves. School failure is nearly always linked to the poverty in which the students and their parents exist. We may never, by ourselves, right the wrongs created by centuries of racism and uncaring individualism. Educators, however, cannot wait for politicians to fulfill their moral obligation; we must do what we can with what we have. Schools have the power to make a difference in the direction this nation's society takes by structuring a new system of schooling, one that is based on what we know can ensure both an effective workforce for the global age and citizens who can live and flourish in the global village. This is indeed our moral obligation.

PART I

FAILING TO CATCH THE NEXT WAVE OF CIVILIZATION

In part I, I argue that we have fallen behind much of the world in regards to preparing our citizens for the global village. Will Rogers was reported to have said that "Even if you're on the right track, you'll get run over if you just stand there." The United States has fallen behind because we have simply kept the same model of schooling left over from the industrial age.

As civilization proceeded into the later twentieth century, public schools remained entrenched in the past. Educators as well as the general public were aware that something had changed—yet were not quite sure exactly what. Our only action was inaction and, worse still, a futile attempt to return to a time that never existed—a time when schools were perceived to educate everyone in our society. Even if we accept that past schooling efforts succeeded in preparing students for the industrial age, which was their intent, they did not prepare minorities or the majority of the underclasses. Those who were fortunate to have left schooling ready for the now-defunct industrial age were actually being left behind.

Sensing failure but ignorant of its causes, we in the United States attempt to recapture "glory" by forcing schooling to return to its former self, a self that was insufficient fifty years ago and is frightfully dangerous today. Basking in ignorance, educators continue down the same worn path. Neoliberals and neoconservatives alike have forced education to reverse itself with the stifling mandates of the accountability movement (Apple 2000). These have caused schools to spiral into irrele-

21

vance. In the next three chapters, I describe the disastrous results of the accountability movement, and then briefly defend the development of global schooling by exploring the third wave of civilization. Finally, I discuss the powers that control schooling and what their intentions may be.

ONE

Accountability in U.S. Schools

The public, influenced by media and politicians at all levels, distrusts our nation's schools, especially those schools that are not in their own communities. This "culture of distrust" emanates, in part, from the many social injustices and inequities of our society. Although schools, as they are now structured and funded, are no more than "mirrors of society," they are nonetheless used as the scapegoats for many of our ills. This culture of distrust regarding schooling has spurred the accountability movements of the latter part of the last century that continue on into this one. At the same time, our schools have been perpetuators of the status quo, at times ensuring that people of certain races, ethnicities, and social standing remain disempowered.

In this chapter, I intend to make sense of how our schools have become irrelevant to both the present and the future. This irrelevancy did not occur overnight. As in the tale of the boiling frog, we educators have not sensed the water becoming hotter. Instead, we have been standing motionless in the pot of water that is civilization until it is too late to save ourselves. I contend, however, that it is *not* too late—at least not yet. As we lie motionless in the boiling water, powerful forces have sprung up around us demanding there be change in schools. Unfortunately, these changes are not actual changes inasmuch as they are simply demands to do more of the same things that schools have been doing for a century or longer. Very few people in this great nation of ours comprehend any other way of schooling our children. Toffler (1970) claimed, and I concur, that the vast majority of people cannot understand that civilization has changed, and that it has fundamentally changed three times in the 8,000 years of human civilization. It takes generations for most people to come to the realization that change has

23

occurred. To meet the demands of this new wave of civilization, we must find a new model for schooling. Some very good ones exist, and the model I describe in the following chapters uses parts of the best models of the past few decades.

What we need even more than a good model, however, is the *marketing* of the need for a new model of schooling to all of schooling's stakeholders—which is practically every aspect of society. We are all connected to schooling and its effects, one way or another. All of us, educators and noneducators alike, need to understand that a better way to educate our children must be found, and that the current reforms are not only useless but are, in fact, dangerous.

Although I do not wish to bore the reader with a detailed recounting of the history of American education, I will briefly highlight some of the major incidents that initiated school reform and our society's reactions to these incidents. Reforms, for the most part, are not the result of occurrences inside the schooling community, but outside. One such incident was the launching of Sputnik in 1957. The Soviet Union's success in being the first nation to penetrate space caused a much-needed introspection by our nation's leaders. We were losing ground to the hated communists; their conquering of space, our nation's leaders feared, could indicate to the rest of the world that their forms of government and economics were superior to ours.

The Soviet Union's success damaged us in two major ways. First, space was and is a militarily strategic entity. The Cold War could have been quickly lost if the Soviets controlled space. The Sputnik launch also damaged our pride, as we could not boast that we were the leaders in the field of space exploration, arguably the most sophisticated area of technological innovation. Who was to blame for our falling behind the communists? Schools were blamed. U.S. schools were not producing enough scientists and mathematicians to win the space race. According to conservative thinkers, the reason was simple: those darned progressives—such as John Dewey—had allowed schools to become "soft" because they were more concerned with socializing than with teaching children the facts. What to do? Ensure more emphasis was given to science and math in the public school and, of course, a return to the "basics." This was done through modest media campaigns and, more important, through a plethora of federal initiatives. The results were several federal programs to increase math and science test scores that were hoped would prove to the world that we could beat the despised communists in the race into space.

In 1961, John F. Kennedy, social liberal yet staunch communist hater, challenged the nation to put a man on the moon by the end of the decade. This was, of course, accomplished—but could schools take the credit? And were they given the credit? Of course not—and perhaps they did not deserve it. The new initiatives to increase math and science test scores did not even have time to affect the works of NASA scientists who had been schooled many years, if not decades, earlier.

Another great moment in recent school reform came twenty years later with the Ronald Reagan–appointed investigation of American schools in the early 1980s. The result was *A Nation at Risk* (National Commission on Excellence in Education 1983), which "proved" to Americans that our school systems were nothing but a series of compromises by teachers. Teachers allowed students to do nothing if the students agreed not to make teachers teach. Well, that is a bit of an exaggeration, but essentially that is what the report led us to believe. The impetus for this investigation, it must be noted, was to discover why the United States was losing ground economically to nations such as Japan, West Germany, and other industrialized countries. Our nation's failure to remain economically dominant was, of course, the schools' fault. Let us examine briefly what was actually happening in the American economy in the early 1980s.

Japan, Germany, and most of Europe were war-torn shells of their former selves after World War II. In Japan, General Douglas MacArthur did what he believed to be prudent in rebuilding the nation by focusing on its economy. To his credit, he summoned W. Edwards Deming from Bell Laboratories to spearhead this rebuilding. Deming and other top American economic theorists (Deming was a statistician) developed a vision that would lead Japan out of its postwar economic depression in not one year or even one decade, but in generations. His now-famous approach was Total Quality Management (TQM) in which he proposed that if a company focused on quality, production and marketing success would take care of themselves. Since 1980 or so, Deming's system has been greatly respected in the business community, but he and TQM were ridiculed in the 1940s, '50s, and '60s by American industry. A focus on quality *and* the customer? No, said U.S. industry, the focus should be on short-term, bottom-line success. Deming, who became nearly godlike to the Japanese, took advantage of the collaborative inclinations of the Japanese to establish teaming in industry as well as a long-term approach to success. By the 1970s, "Made in Japan" had gone from meaning that a product was junk to implying a high level of quality (Deming 1986).

American industry, still not admitting fault, blamed U.S. laborers and their unions for our economic woes; laborers were, they would have the public believe, lazy and "money grubbing." Poor work ethics (often attributed to schools being lax in discipline) were the reasons why the United States was losing ground to the Japanese and Germans. It was not until the late 1970s and early 1980s that quality became the centerpiece of most American industries. The fault for declining world market share lay not with the schools (which were simply doing what they were asked to do—that is, prepare students to work in the factories of the industrial age) but with American industrial management practices. The focus on short-term profit and the use of external rewards for workers had caught up with U.S. industry. Deming (1986) and his colleagues had developed a new model across the Pacific, a model that was enormously successful. By the time U.S. companies finally realized the problem and began to implement quality management, much of the world economy had become globalized; the Japans and Germanys of the world had caught and even surpassed the United States in many economic factors, exemplified by the trade deficit. No longer would the United States dominate the industrial world. (Admittedly, globalization was inevitable, but the United States' industrial demise of the 1970s and '80s was hastened by our reliance on poor management practices.)

The economic woes of the United States in the 1970s and '80s cannot be blamed on U.S. schools. Nor, for that matter, can economic success be directly attributed to schools. Education reformers used the remainder of the 1980s to devise ways to increase standardized test scores, a wasteful endeavor. The 1980s reforms would not have an impact on learning—assuming that they ever did—until at least the mid to late 1990s. Yet, by 1993, the American economy had begun to climb out of the recession. The economic boom of the 1990s was particularly linked to one industry: technology, especially computer-related products and services. The computer boom was not, however, a result of the 1980s back-to-basics school reforms. With the possible exception of the G.I. Bill of the 1940s, it is unlikely any educational reform has greatly affected the American economy. At least so far, using schools as scapegoats for a poor economy, as was done in *A Nation at Risk*, is erroneous; it is merely political fodder for the political right as well as the left. However, if we continue to train citizens to be nothing more than industrial-age workers, then indeed schools should accept at least part of the blame.

WHAT ACCOUNTABILITY REALLY DOES TO SCHOOLS

I believe it essential that we examine the motives and results of the accountability movement that began in the 1980s. *A Nation at Risk* warned of economic peril if our schools were not placed onto the right track. Indeed, they were on the right track, only they just stood still until they were run over, as Will Rogers warned. Schools were relatively unchanged by the 1990s when the economy experienced its longest continuous upswing in history. If holding schools accountable for student learning to ensure national economic success is useless, then why do we or should we hold schools accountable? Well, it is the job of educators to help students learn (what they learn and how they learn is a matter of great debate) to be successful in their lives, and that in itself is reason enough to continue to hold educators accountable for student learning. The public, however, rarely examines the actual results of the accountability movement itself but only studies the results—SAT scores, school rankings, etc.—that the accountability movement self-reports.

For students, the accountability movement has meant more time on task (although the tasks are often inane and mundane) and an increased number and higher standards to be attained. For teachers, this translates to more stringent licensure and certification and ensuring that students meet the standards. And what are the standards and who establishes them? Who dictates licensure and certification requirements for teachers? Both depend on which state you are in, as these are established and controlled at a state level and are theoretically different for each state. (At the time of this writing, Iowa was the only state that did not have standards for students, yet Iowa often has the highest SAT scores among all fifty states!) Some states have reciprocity for teacher licensure or certification so a teacher can more easily move from one state into another without having to take a myriad of courses and mind-numbing staff development training to be able to teach in their adopted state, but many states do not have this reciprocity. The difference between licensure and certification is simply that education officials and politicians believe that the term "licensure" sounds more rigorous to the public; therefore, many states are requiring a bit "more of the same" of their teachers and are changing the terminology.

Standards, as well as benchmarks, are theoretically good ideas. I use the term "theoretically" because although many see them as well intended—a way to ensure increased learning in all schools—what most do not see is that they could be (and are, in some cases) political weapons used to dismantle and privatize public schooling. A strong yet accurate statement, I am afraid. As noted earlier, Florida's whole system of "crime and punishment" (that is, its accountability movement with its bribing and retributions) is fast becoming the national model, influencing all states. If schools do not ensure that students reach the changing standards (states like to boast that they continue to "raise the bar"), then they will lose their students and have their faculty and administration reassigned or fired. In a worst-case scenario, this makes way for privatization or the "McDonaldization" of schooling based on national standards and teacher-proof curricula where anyone can open up shop and hire uneducated "teachers" to baby-sit students while they slog through prepackaged test preparation "curricula." This type of schooling falls in line with the "annual yearly progress" segment of the Elementary and Secondary Education Act (ESEA) meant to ensure that all students reach a certain level of learning before moving on to the next grade level or school. This McDonaldization resembles an assembly line where a bolt is tightened at one stop and a widget is added at the next. The idea seems to be that all products . . . I mean, children . . . will be alike; each and every adolescent will come out of high school with the same knowledge akin to each McDonald's hamburger being the same when served to you at the counter. Children, alas, are not products but people. The factory model of schooling requires that each student be treated as an inanimate object. See chapters 2 and 3 for more information on this unacceptable model of schooling.

Standards are intended to produce predictable outcomes. Innovation and individuality are lost in the standards process. The fact that standards are measured by standardized testing helps keep schooling from changing. Typically, low-level learning is stressed while collaborative, intuitive project learning is discouraged because the latter cannot be assessed using a standardized pencil-and-paper test. Teachers teach to the test and, frankly, I can't blame them. As a secondary school assistant principal, another administrator and I conducted a workshop for our school's 200 teachers on the state-mandated examination—how it was to be structured and how the questions were to be posed. As we did this, we also had to explain that our district's stance was that teachers should not concentrate on increased test scores, a stance with which I heartily agreed. Yet, we also had to inform them that if our students' scores were high enough, our school would receive $100 for each of our 3,600 students. Our hearts may have been in the right place, but our brains could easily calculate the size of our governor's bribe. The governor's carrot-and-stick approach prevailed; our teachers spent much time preparing our students for the test, the students did well, and our school pocketed a great amount of money to be spent however we saw fit. We decided to buy more computers for the students. Being a school with a relatively high socioeconomic level, we had quite a few computers already; the low SES schools (assuming their lower test results) received nothing. Thus, the rich got richer and the poor got bad publicity from the media. Eventually, teachers and school-based administrators in our state either became greedy or wanted to spite the governor's attack on teachers unions, which had not supported his election. School personnel opted to keep this money as bonuses. How much did that help students? And what about schools with low grades due to low test scores? After two years of failure (receiving an F score), their students are free to abandon these neighborhood schools to go to another public school or even a private school. Private schools, according to urban legend, are superior to public schools in every way. According to research, however, this is merely a legend—especially when SES is controlled.

The standards movement, a result of the accountability movement, requires teachers to simply do more of the same—more "skill and drill" instead of learning that requires deep understanding, the learning that enables students to succeed in the global economy and in the global village of ever-changing cultural and social environments. Teaching to the test is the primary function of our public schools, a practice from which our children and our society will suffer. Standardized testing allows for the accumulation of data that can and are used to punish teachers and schools as well as students. It is my opinion that states are adopting the Florida A+ model that awards grades to schools based mostly on their students' scores on the Florida Comprehensive Assessment Test. Much of the spirit of the A+ plan is found in the ESEA. When the A+ plan was first put into effect, the grade the school received was based on other data besides FCAT scores, data such as attendance and dropout rate. The state eventually settled on two main criteria: test scores and increases in those scores. A school awarded an A received a great amount of publicity *and* money. Those schools that received an F were not only attacked by the media and the governor's office but the students in the schools had the opportunity to go to any other school of their choice, including private schools. Because I was at an A school, I found that parents were knocking at our door wanting to see if their children could attend and receive some of the "magic" our school had to offer. This lasted for only a year or so, as parents and students were quick to discover that it was not the quality of teaching taking place in the "successful" schools but the SES of the children that mattered. (My apologies to the hard-working former colleagues of mine at this school.) It can be easily predicted which schools will receive high scores on standardized tests simply by reading their free- and reduced-price lunch percentages. Those with the least poverty will likely succeed.

The Florida A+ plan, despite the Florida governor's praises, is a complete failure in regards to educating children. It is a success, however, in turning schools into test-taking factories. It also has failed so far in meeting with what I suspect is the governor's hidden agenda: privatizing all public schools with the use of vouchers (or its market name, "opportunity scholarships") awarded to students in schools that receive low grades. Parents, as noted above, have learned that teachers are usually very good no matter where they are (at least in promoting the industrial-age schooling agenda); the challenges of teaching become greater the lower the SES of that school. In short, students did not flee the public schools in Florida. The entrepreneurs, waiting like vultures ready to open storefront private "schools for profit" while feasting on public money, are still waiting. The existing private schools knew already that vouchers were not going to be enough for them to accept children of poverty, nor were they likely to have the knowledge, skills, and resources to educate the masses of students coming from poverty.

The pinnacle of the accountability and subsequent standards movement came in 2001 when a political compromise was struck between Democrats in Congress and the Bush administration, an agreement that ironically compromised the future of our schools and our children. The Elementary and Secondary Education Act of 2001 (ESEA), better known as No Children Left Behind (or, as many educators refer to it, "No Child Left Untested") established that schools would be held accountable to ensure that (1) all students continuously increase their learning; that one year in school will translate to one year's learning, (2) all teachers will be "highly qualified," and (3) or else! The "or else" is that the states will be forced to do something drastic about a failing school (i.e., one where students do not do well on the mandated tests) and teachers who are not highly qualified as measured by suspect teacher examinations.

Continuously Learning Students

Let us explore what is meant by "continuously learning" to those who support the accountability movement. Student success is currently measured by test scores that are developed, controlled, and funded by each state. Like robots, our children are expected to be at a certain level at a certain time as evidenced by test scores. First, even if these tests were valid (and I contend they are not), how can one expect a human being to go through the assembly line of our factory-model schools and expect to learn a "year's worth of knowledge" each and every year? Just considering the variables of a child's life both inside and outside of the school is mind-boggling: What the child ate or did not eat the day of the test. How much sleep the child had the night before the test. Where the child slept the night before (in a car with his or her homeless family?). What happened to the child throughout the entire school year. How many times the child moved in and out of his or her home, or his or her school. Whether or not the child was a victim of some sort of scarring abuse. We could go on forever. Each of these variables renders the test results invalid, or at least suspect. But how else can we measure a student's learning besides these high-stakes tests (by "high stakes," I refer to any tests that can affect a child's school career or a school)? Educators for years have advocated authentic assessment, which is a conglomeration of many different assessments that are more in tune with what the child actually knows, based on real-life applications of knowledge. How often are we asked to take paper-and-pencil tests at our workplace to prove we are worthy of our job? Or in our homes with our family to prove we are worthy of being a family member? How about in our community to prove that we are worthy of being in that community? One can see the absurdity of this constant testing.

Contrary to what it may seem, I am not against all testing. I actually feel that *some* testing is very useful for teachers to help in determining students' needs. The problem I have with testing is when it becomes high stakes, used as a weapon (and not a tool) for the teacher and the parents. My contention is that no one is better equipped at assessing a student's learning than that student's teacher or teachers. A once-a-year test only assesses how well a child performs on that one test, on a given day. But, alas, we cannot allow teachers to assess their students' learning because we all know from the media and the supporters of the ESEA that teachers are not qualified to do so! This erroneous belief emanates from our culture of distrust, developed over the past generation or two.

Highly Qualified Teachers

All teachers should indeed be highly qualified. Who would argue with that? Some critics claim that teachers' unions try to protect incompetent teachers and, perhaps, this may sometimes be the case. However, I do believe that these unions desire to have all teachers as highly competent and qualified as possible. What is "highly qualified" when referring to teachers depends on the state, as noted earlier. The ESEA allows for each state to make that determination, which means a highly qualified teacher in Florida could be a completely incompetent teacher in Ohio. Qualifications are based on certification or licensure unique to each state, despite reciprocity between some states. Some systems developed by national organizations are being embraced across a multitude of states.

This helps standardized teacher certification and licensure, but does it ensure teacher quality? You cannot standardize quality. Quality is subjective and relative to many circumstance and variables. Still, a teacher may prove to be of high quality to one student but not to another because that teacher's style is not congruent with the second child's learning style. The developers of the Praxis system, as well as other teacher evaluation systems, will rightfully tell you that their system is based on sound research. A blanket assessment of teachers cannot, however, determine if a teacher is highly qualified.

So how can this assessment be made? Well, how do we assess whether or not our physician or our carpenter is highly qualified? Each has a license. Fine. Physicians most certainly have a medical degree and other degrees from institutions of higher learning, but the true measure of their qualification is in their work, and who judges their work? We, the consumers, do. The consumers for teachers, if you will, are the parents and the students. Why not allow them to assess if the teacher is highly qualified? If there is any doubt, have the teacher's peers and administrators assess. These last two assessments cannot be made by one-time observations but through a long-term multifaceted assessment of the teacher's work with children—a fair and just outcomes-based accountability.

PUNISHING FOR SUCCESS?

Let us also examine more closely the "or else," as this seems to be at the core of the accountability movement. If schools that are determined by the state to be low achieving for two years, the ESEA states that parents have the right to transfer their child from the low-achieving school to another school in the same district that is high achieving. An effort has been made in some states to allow for students to move into schools in other districts. If a school is low achieving or "fails" for three years in a row, then parents of children in that school are allowed Title

I federal money to purchase supplemental services, such as Sylvan and other for-profit tutoring companies.

There are problems with this scenario. Let us say that 75 percent of the parents in failing school X move their children to high-achieving schools Y and Z. How will the other two schools fit all those new students into their buildings? And where are all the new teachers going to come from? School X, of course. It is unlikely that schools Y and Z will be able to hire new faculty from outside the district. Furthermore, why was school X failing to begin with? Most likely, the children were from low socioeconomic homes (assuming they are not homeless). Are the children from school X going to somehow overcome all learning barriers that are a result of society's inequities simply by transferring schools? Of course not. It is a solid assumption that all three of these schools are essentially the same in curriculum and teacher quality; the only factor for school X's failure is that its students are underprivileged. Granted, it is conceivable that schools Y and Z may indeed have higher quality teachers; unfortunately, they most likely will not know how to work with underprivileged children if their students have always been from middle-class homes.

What happens to school X when most of the students have left? Most likely, the majority of the most academically successful of the students, at least those who have caring parents, will bother to move schools. This means that school X will be left with the children least likely to learn and will probably be left with the teachers the other schools did not want. That school will have to be shut down. Then what? All the children will be given "opportunity scholarships" to go to private schools. Vouchers are typically not enough for most highly regarded private schools to accept as full tuition and chances are that private schools would not accept someone, or at least keep someone, who has difficulty learning due to societal deprivation. (How would the parents transport the child to the new private school if free transportation is not provided? Going back to the scenario of schools X, Y, and Z, what if the district has *no* successful schools? Will the parents be able to transport the child to another district's schools?)

In honor of those who worship the marketplace, I will employ a tired, worn-out expression: the bottom line; and that bottom line is, schools are being forced to fail. Michael Apple in *Educating the "Right" Way*

(2001) refers to the widespread belief in the standards movement as "conservative modernization" (an oxymoron?). This belief is due to the resounding success of the theory that the only way to fix schools is with relentless testing and strict accountability measures. The current Bush administration reaped the benefit of conservative modernization by its ability to pass the ESEA with few concessions to Democrats. The Democratic Party, which seems to have no better view of effective schooling than what has been done and is still being done (that is, industrial-age, factory-style schooling), is forced to follow the consensus of the people, supporting conservative modernization.

The publicized focus of conservative modernization and subsequently the ESEA is to increase learning and teacher quality. No mention is made of changing the schooling process itself. (To its credit and the generosity of the Gates Foundation, the schools-within-schools model is being advanced.) The results of this movement is simply to do more of the same—more of what schools have been doing for decades, if not centuries. The hidden agenda of conservative modernization is indeed hidden to most of us in education, and is often denied by both educators and noneducators: the complete privatization of schooling. The assumption is that private schools are far superior to public schools, but studies consistently suggest that when SES is controlled, public and private school success are practically equal as measured by test scores. Why, then, would anyone promote privatization of schools? Simply put, it fits with the philosophy of smaller government, stronger markets. Yet, schools-for-profit have yet to prove successful, nor has any system of vouchers to date. "Conservative modernizers," to borrow Apple's term, seem convinced that privatizing every aspect of our government will somehow rectify society's woes. Although competition has its benefits, powerful government at all levels needs to exist to ensure equitable (not equal!) treatment of all. An unbridled market system, as exemplified by recent corporate scandals, can wreak havoc throughout the economy and our society.

Two

Waves of Civilization

Alvin Toffler (1980) proposed over twenty years ago that we are living in a new wave of civilization, an age that is vastly different from the previous two waves (agricultural and industrial). This new wave is one that we, as a nation and as educators, do not quite yet understand. Our minds are still set in the industrial age of factories and bureaucratic organizations and we view our schools and schooling through the lens of the second wave of civilization that ended in the United States about fifty years ago.

When humans started cultivating crops and domesticating animals, they began to abandon their hunting and gathering ways. Civilizations arose from small bands of farmers who found they no longer needed to follow game in order to survive. This was the first wave of civilization, the age of agriculture. It dominated humankind for 8,000 years, until first Europe and then North America began industrializing in the eighteenth and nineteenth centuries. Compulsory schooling in the United States, a concept developed in New England, coincided with the industrialization of America. Laws were passed to ensure that all could read the Bible so that they could ward off the devil; one such law was even called the Old Deluder Act. By the mid-nineteenth century, Americans understood that they must educate en masse, as immigrants flocked to the United States and needed to learn to read and write English as well as to become successfully anglicized.

STUCK IN THE PAST

"Education for all" was instituted to accommodate the needs of the factory, a by-product of the industrial age. Workforce skills in the second

37

wave differed greatly from the agricultural age. Time and subservience were the new foci. Students were taught to take orders from supervisors, to be prompt so that the assembly line would not be missing a "cog" and production could commence according to the master plan, and to be content with the repetitive performance of mind-numbingly simple tasks. This was the general plan of public schooling then, and still is today. Teachers, administrators, tight schedules, accountability measures, and quality controls mandated by politicians dominate the actions of students. So do a myriad of rules accompanied by "zero tolerance" consequences.

For generations, students merely had to learn these rules and abide by them for twelve to thirteen years and they would be awarded a high school diploma. This was not always the case. Perhaps high schools prior to the 1960s and '70s were more stringent in their requirements, but they did not need to worry about dropout rates. An eighth-grade education was quite sufficient for most industrial-age jobs; perhaps one needed only a fourth- or fifth-grade education. As the workforce began to be saturated in the late 1950s and early '60s, the movement to keep children in school strengthened. Focusing on dropout rates served the dual purpose of keeping teenagers out of the workforce for a few years, allowing unemployed adults to find work, and kept teenagers off the streets. To this day, most crime is committed in the few hours in the afternoon between school dismissal and when parents typically come home from work—proof that schools still serve their purpose of keeping children and adolescents out of trouble, for at least a few hours a day (statistics suggest that juvenile crime is dramatically higher in non-school hours during the week (OJJDP, 1999)).

The agricultural age did not abruptly end a few centuries ago; it slowly retreated until farm workers became a very small slice of the American workforce. The need for formal learning was not great in this age, especially in predominantly rural areas, at least not until the last 50–100 years. Abraham Lincoln is a perfect example. He had about one year of formal schooling in southern Indiana as his family made their way from Kentucky to Illinois. Learning to read was the gateway for this self-taught attorney and politician. If Lincoln had been raised in an urban area in the Northeast, however, it is unlikely that he could have succeeded in his profession without a formalized education, even in the mid-1800s. (Mark Twain, though, is supposed to have said that the only profession that has no prerequisite knowledge or experience is that of the politician.) Today, of course, farmers need to be highly educated in order to succeed in the complicated and competitive agriculture industry of the twenty-first century. And today, our sixteenth president would need an additional eighteen years of formal schooling just to practice law in his hometown of Springfield, Illinois. To become president, however, it can be argued that one needs only the right combination of charisma, money, and connections. The curricula of formal education seem to have little to do with preparing one for the office of president. This would invalidate the motivation used by teachers and parents for over a century: study hard and some day you can become president.

As the agricultural age faded into the industrial age, factory-style schooling replaced the "little red schoolhouse." Secondary schools, especially, became factory-like in both organization and culture, where principals supervised teachers who, in turn, supervised students. Central school offices formed in cities to supervise principals and, of course, school boards oversaw the workings of everyone, although by design they are to make policy, not manage the everyday activities of schools—a fact historically overlooked by overzealous school board members. Urban school systems became giant pyramids of bureaucracy with layer upon layer of staff, with the school board and superintendent at the pinnacle and the student at the bottom of the pile.

School systems enacted centralized curricula that often interfered with teachers' work in the classroom. Teachers were seen as automated deliverers of knowledge, and that knowledge came from the textbooks upon which the teachers were forced to rely. Children were mere cogs in the machine called school. They were to sit passively and absorb knowledge transferred to them from the textbooks via the teachers. This passivity was valued greatly in the factory where workers were asked not to think, but only to arrive promptly, obey their line foreman, and perform mundane tasks over and over again. Teachers modeled the job of factory supervisor, as that was their primary task: supervision. As more and more students were stuffed into each classroom, classroom supervision and management surpassed in importance the job of transmitting content. Students who had witnessed firsthand the supervising powers of their teachers would, it was reasoned, respond to line supervisors in the factory or to the management in other bureaucratic organizations.

The line worker and the line supervisors were educated in the factory-style public schools. The company executives, on the other hand, had often been educated in private preparatory schools that would lead them to a distinguished university. In the private schools, students were controlled not by the school system, as was the intention of the public schools, but by social expectations. Private schools were a means to an end, the end being a professional career and high social standing. This was the birthright of the wealthy. The only worthwhile school reform, the G.I. Bill, allowed mostly working-class men to enter colleges. This began to reshape the culture of upper management because this new class of managers brought with them their own cultural values. This time period (the 1950s and '60s) coincided with the onset of the third wave of civilization. Toffler (1980) notes that in 1955, for the first time, more than half of the U.S. workforce was white-collar management or professional class in contrast to blue-collar laborers. This, he believes, signaled the beginning of the end of the second wave and spurred the growth of the technological age/information age/global age. (The terminology has changed over the years; I have settled upon "global age.") One has to wonder how long this third wave will last, what the next wave will be like, and what will be expected of those who live and work in it. I am confident that futurists such as Toffler have spent much time and grey matter pondering the realities of the future, and an understanding of it will benefit us all. I would, however, be satisfied if we could simply come to understand the needs and expectations of the third wave in which we now reside.

CLASS WARFARE

The wealthy and upper-middle classes often receive a different education from those in the lower classes, as mentioned in the previous section. Beginning in the middle of the last century, knowledge became power, and those who had knowledge and could understand the needs of the present and the future became the most powerful. Many of the traits necessary to succeed in the economy of the global age are passed on by the powerful to their children. The British business scholar Charles Handy argues in *The Age of Paradox* (1995) that the upper classes of society ensure that their children obtain the "Three C's": conceptualizing, coordinating, and consolidating. He contends, and I concur, that these skills are not adequately fostered in the public schools. If they are addressed at all, they are simply add-ons to the curricula that consist mostly of facts or "nouns," as Handy refers to them. The Three C's are active verbs that allow students to know what to do with the nouns. Simply knowing facts and regurgitating them onto a test, or "bulimic education," offers nothing of substance to the students and society. Wealthy families ensure that their children are educated to use the nouns by understanding how to employ the verbs. This education usually comes through experiences offered to the students by their families, not the schools. The lower classes have neither the resources nor the understanding (due to lack of experiences) of what these verbs are or how to use them; therefore, the majority of publicly educated students leave schools unprepared to really make a difference in society and the postindustrial world. They are essentially left behind.

How can schools make up for this difference in experience? Handy wisely insists that the verbs should be the core of the curriculum. I agree, but how would we do this? The standards movement began by attempting to establish what students should know, do, and be like. The "know" *might* be fairly assessed by standardized tests. (I might be giving credit where it is not due, as most test items measure very low-level learning, as described by Benjamin Bloom in his famous Taxonomy of Learning [1956].) Testing does not assess what students can do and what they are like. Instead, a qualitative and, perhaps, somewhat subjective assessment must be administered to discover what students can do and what they are like when they leave school. Teachers would have to establish activities where students can demonstrate what they are able to do; many progressive-thinking teachers do this already. They would also need to gain a deep understanding of what the students are like— something that is impossible in the factory-style school structures that exist where secondary, and even many intermediate-level elementary, teachers have 100 to 150 or more students.

Even if we were to restructure schools so that teachers could actually get to know their students, how could we come up with the quantitative data that would get the attention of the media? The media and politicians have been feeding on numbers that signify the failure of schools (e.g., dropout percentages, proficiency test failure percentages, the absurd grading of public schools). Without "hard data"—that is, numbers—how can we hold schools accountable? My argument is that numbers do not tell the whole story and, of course, can be easily manipulated to make a case for any side someone wants to take. What cannot be manipulated as easily is a teacher's assessment of a student based on social and professional contact with that student. Dialoguing and sharing experiences allow for someone to know another person. This is the only way we can fully understand what a student can do and be like. The Swedes understand this, and so do others, as I will point out when I later present a model for schooling in the global age.

The learning of the Three C's by the upper classes ensures their domination of other classes and the perpetuation of their family's power and position. The underclasses depend on schools to prepare their children for the future but, alas, the schools their children attend provide them with outdated skills. These skills, accompanied by the lack of the Three C's, relegate the majority of the underclasses to low-wage, dead-end jobs. Public schooling, in its present state, ensures that the children of the underclasses will receive low-level education and, in turn, will continue to be controlled by the powerful so that the powerful can continue their dominance.

It is morally essential that we create equitable models of schooling so that anyone, not just those with great advantages, can succeed and contribute to our economy and our society—and not merely as chattel under the direction of the rich and powerful.

MAKING SENSE OF THE THIRD WAVE

The third wave is not easily understood because, as Toffler (1980) contends, we are unable to completely comprehend the wave in which we live until after the last wave has disappeared. In other words, only "hindsight is 20/20." People tend to cling to what they already know (i.e., tradition) because it is comfortable and causes little conflict of thought. Globalization scholars warn against those who would take the world backward. They cite religious fundamentalists around the world as examples of those who battle the inevitable changes in the world order, fundamentalists such as the al Qaeda of the Muslim faith and the Zapatistas in Mexico (Castells 2000). One must also include the relatively benign religious fundamentalists in our own nation who would take us back to a "better world," one that included racially separate and unequal schools (well, maybe they would not have to go back in time to find these), Jim Crow laws, the slaughter of Native Americans, and the unequal treatment of women (all of which continue to persist). These reactionaries view the past through the proverbial rose-colored glasses, but essentially what they see and long for are the days when white men were all-powerful and the written and unwritten laws of society were enforced to keep it that way.

Fundamentalists have a great hold on schools (see chapter 3 for more information on that topic). They see their own schooling as being far superior to today's. What they do not see in their "perfect past" are the grotesque realities of segregated schools, the enormous dropout rates, and the irrelevant education that they received—that is, irrelevant to the present global age. I must refer back to the school board meeting in Sweden mentioned in the introduction. The adults in the audience were reminded by the Swedish principal that their school experiences had little or no relevance to what was happening in the schools of today (or at least in her community's schools). The adults were educated for the industrial age and, I should add, if American adults completed compulsory schooling after 1955, their education was obsolete even upon graduation, if Toffler's timing of the end of the industrial age is correct. To take schools back to a "golden age" is ludicrous, considering the past was not golden. Unfortunately, it is this dream of a golden age that is holding schools back.

Organized labor can be added to this list of reactionaries longing for better days gone by. Yes, I am a believer in the spirit of organized labor, as laborers would have very few elected officials willing to act on their behalf if they did not have the power to organize. The plight of the working class would be in a much, much worse state without organized labor. In order to increase their power, labor must play the role of special interest group in order to gain any attention in Washington, D.C. If labor did not participate in this "buying of votes" scheme that powers politics, then the rich would indeed be even more powerful and wealthier than they are.

I add labor to this list of reactionaries because they, too, wish to go back to a time when it seemed much better for them. With the devastation of Europe after World War II, the United States was the only powerful economy on the globe. Despite wasteful and hurtful management practices based on Frederick Taylor's time studies of the early twentieth century, U.S. business flourished due to this lack of global competition. Labor could ask for and get nearly anything it wanted, thanks in part to the postwar economic boom and the decades of struggle by labor unions. As a result, labor received great increases in external motivators (pay, benefits) and a continuance of poor internal motivators (and increases in demotivators) that includes, but is not limited to, poor relationships between labor and management. Improving the relationships between labor and management, and allowing for more autonomy in the workplace that includes more decision making by all, could have increased productivity without requiring industry to greatly increase the pay scales.

The result was and is a terrific rift between labor and management, where management was allowed to keep all the real power in the organizations. If sharing power had been the result of the labor movement after World War II instead of increasing external motivators, then perhaps management would not have been able to cunningly increase executive compensation to astronomical levels. Labor simply demanded and received the external motivators of pay and benefits without seeking shared decision making, which would have allowed them to share power with the powerful.

What labor would like, and I cannot blame them, is a return to the days when they could ask and receive tremendous increases in compensation. Unfortunately, the world has passed them by. Globalization has rendered their tactics useless. Go on strike? Go ahead; management will simply move production to a Third World nation. If labor had been able to garner real power in industry instead of merely demanding and receiving external motivators, then they could be in a position to make the decisions about where production would take place and how much the chief executive officer could earn.

I must clarify that I am not a proponent of globalization, merely a student of it. I agree with most globalization scholars that we can do little—if anything—to stop it. We can only steer it toward a more just society. As it stands, globalization is in the hands of the powerful. Major corporations that were initially based in the United States have internationalized so that they can better reap the benefits of globalization without being limited by nation-states. No longer do some national governments hold the power to dictate their own economies. This is done by the multinational corporations who have no allegiance to any nation, only to stockholders and executives. (Although in light of the Enron, Tyco, and Global Crossing scandals of recent years, one must wonder about executives' relationships with their stockholders!) Their only commitment may be increased compensation for upper management while turning their backs on their workers and their nation's people. Why else would they go to great measures to set up faux offices overseas in order to avoid taxation that would, in turn, benefit "their" nation and its people?

As I describe a system of schooling that will prepare our students and the United States for the global age, I refer to what I witnessed in Sweden. The Swedes were able to take nearly every progressive education notion and strategy and implement them nationwide. As I examined this implementation, I pondered how we Americans could do the same. One of the results of this progressivism in the schools was the happiness of the students and the people about their schools. (I oversimplify for effect, but relative to the United States, the people seemed quite satisfied with their nation's schools.) As I delved deeper into the Swedish culture, their nationalized curricula, and the impact immigration has had on the nation, I came to the conclusion that we could not replicate much of what I had seen, or at least it would not be nearly as easy as it was for the Swedes because of one factor: poverty. The Swedes, in comparison to America, had eradicated poverty. Since World War II, only two nations have consistently closed or stabilized the gap between rich and poor: Sweden and Norway. Interestingly, these are the only two Western nations whose citizens report being happier today than fifty years ago. These societies are quite collectivist as compared to ours, a topic that will be discussed in chapter 5.

Nearly all the problems in U.S. schools are directly related to poverty: inequity in learning and funding, violence, and students' reluctance to learn. I will not go into detail at this time as to how each and every problem is connected to our schools' lack of success, but suffice it to say that without poverty, our jobs as educators would be, as my father often says, "like a Sunday school picnic" compared to what it is today. Who is to blame for our poverty? The villains are many, but our entire way of life must come into question.

At this point, however, I would like the reader to ponder what schools would be like without oppressive poverty. How many of our schools' problems would simply go away? Politicians have the power to wipe out poverty. Instead of using this power, they blame society's ills—ills caused mostly by poverty—on the schools. They give schools the task of educating all children but do not support them financially, as anyone can see from the new No Child Left Behind legislation. However, educators can do much to improve schooling in the United States. As I describe the model of schooling for the global age, I do not include the help of politicians. I do not believe that schooling can immediately change the corruption of power in which our political state exists, and if anything, politicians will work to keep schooling from becoming an institution that promotes empowerment (they have too much to lose if the society actually democratizes). My hope is that if an education system that promotes true democracy is built, the overall American society will be forever changed within a generation or two. Quite a dream, many might think it naive, yet ideas and visions must exist on hope, which I refuse to relinquish.

THREE

Those Who Control Schooling

A great amount of history has been written about the purposes of compulsory public education. Essentially, most Americans believed (and still believe) that schools should prepare children for their future. It is difficult to ascertain what the future holds, or for that matter, what the present world requires of its citizens and workers. A global economy is part of this future; unfortunately, a result of this global economy is a monoculture of consumerism that has manifested over much of the developed world. As a reaction to the aforementioned "McDonaldization" of culture, many throughout the world have formed resistances through revived nationalism, fundamental religious zealousness, and other reactionary movements. Some of these movements are found in the United States and are, thankfully, much less violent versions than, say, al Qaeda. These movements—as well as many others—are trying to control our schools and, I believe, succeeding.

Michael Apple (2000) calls the two forces that now control U.S. schooling "neoliberals" and "neoconservatives."

The former wish to make consumers out of our students and, to their credit, prepare better workers. (To their discredit, however, they support schooling that trains the underclasses for low-paying service jobs.) The neoconservatives merely want to have students learn basic industrial-age knowledge—knowledge that will not prepare them to succeed, let alone survive, in the global economy or in the global village. Fundamental religious factions, proponents of both neoliberalism and neoconservatism, also wish to instill values—their own religious values, often not congruent with those that will enable citizens to live in a globalized world (Castells, 2000a; Delors, 1998).

Neoliberals believe strongly that schooling's function is to produce a ready workforce. They buy into those parts of the quality movement of school management that require the schools to meet the needs of the client in order for them to offer a quality service. In this, I wholeheartedly agree. As schools bureaucratized, the instructional staff (teachers and administrators) and noninstructional staff cared little about customer service. I have seen secretaries, teachers, and administrators act rudely—devoid of customer service skills—toward parents, families, and other constituents. Critics of education would say that this is due to educators never living in the "real world" of business. Some of this may be true. Tayloristic bureaucracy (from Frederick Taylor) produces a workforce that sees the consumer of its services or products as merely a nuisance. This was evidenced in years past in other monopolistic bureaucracies, such as public utilities companies and the U.S. Postal Service, organizations that had no real competition and, therefore, did not need to concern themselves with customer satisfaction. This situation is not as common as it once was due to implementation of quality management and philosophy in nearly every organization. For the most part, civil servants and workers in monopolies are more aware of the customers' needs and rights. This is true, also, of schools. Just in the past decade, it is my opinion that school front offices have generally become more client-friendly.

However, to change schools only for the sake of making better workers is not seeing the whole picture. I firmly believe that only by fostering citizens who are empowered to learn and live in a real democracy will our citizens have the skills and traits necessary to succeed in the global economy, one that is often volatile and very unpredictable. Industry embraces Total Quality Management where the foci are quality of process and the clients' needs; schools, on the other hand, are infatuated with the end result—that is, paper-and-pencil testing of often mundane knowledge.

In addition, schools' view of the client is ambiguous. If no one can identify the client, then how can we know and attempt to meet the needs of the client? The defining question when implementing quality in schools may be: Who is the client? In business, the client is obviously the consumer and, perhaps, distributors. In schools, this is much more of a gray area. Parents, most educators would agree, are clients of the school systems. Some would say clients also include other stakeholders such as the business community and the outside community as a whole (local, state, regional, national—and, dare I suggest, global?).

A business administration professor I knew insisted that the only client of the schools that really counted was the business community. He argued that schools would not improve unless they paid more attention to what business said it needed from the schools. I agree, but with qualifications. Yes, schools do need to take heed of the needs of business. In sorting through some of the vast literature of what people should know, do, and be like for the global economy, I found that essentially four competencies or skills were paramount: teamwork, pragmatic technological skills, problem solving, and entrepreneurship.

First, I need to clarify to the reader that I do not believe that we live merely to work nor does a society exist with people who are effective only in their jobs. But if our citizens are to be prepared to work in the global economy, we need to know what we as schools can do to help them become successful—not just as low-paid service workers but as highly compensated knowledge workers.

The need for being able to work effectively in a team setting is a direct result of the quality movement. American businesses were impressed with the motivation of Japanese workers and the quality products that resulted in their working collaboratively. This type of working environment requires workers not only to be willing to work with others but also to have certain collaboration skills, such as being able to mediate conflict (negotiating a "win-win" solution rather than fighting for the "win-lose" that is traditional in our competitive American culture). This is closely linked to problem solving of conflict within a group, but the competency of problem solving requires more than resolving interpersonal conflict, or for that matter *intra*personal conflict. It requires being able to resolve complicated problems presented to a team of workers. To use a school/manufacturing example, we can say that "Given that the widget (a teaching strategy) that drives the sprocket (a student's knowledge) in the front-end assembly of the Acme racer (the student) is not reacting properly (according to various assessments), what can the assembly team (educators who work with the student) do to efficiently and effectively fix this?" That is how global organizations function—as a team of problem solvers, which is quite different from American schooling, which is focused almost entirely on the individual taking blame and resolving the problem by him or herself.

Technological expertise is becoming even more essential in the work-force now that computers are an integral part of nearly every worker's life, but other technological expertise exists, such as craftsmanship with the use of highly technical equipment. Still, computer literacy and even expertise cannot be dismissed in the global economy. American schools are working toward increased technological learning, but poorly funded urban and rural schools keep falling further and further behind wealthy suburban and private schools. This lack of technological experiences helps to ensure that those born into the underclasses remain there.

Finally, business leaders and scholars insist that the global economy needs people with entrepreneurial spirit and expertise. Executives in business, as well as any flexible organization that is willing to meet the needs of the client, must be willing to take risks. As the economy re-mains in a state of flux, with no one really able to accurately predict where it is heading, leaders must possess the courage to make difficult decisions, leading their organizations—or facilitating the direction of their organizations—to a place that is unknown. This risk taker must be creative or rely on others who are creative. I hesitate to use the cliché but, yes, they need to, or have others who can, "think outside the box."

Are schools preparing this type of worker? Such strategies as coopera-tive learning encourage collaboration among students. These strategies, although widespread, are not the rule in America's classroom. Too often, the teacher acts as the dispenser of knowledge and the students as the individual receptacles of this "expertise." This knowledge is often extracted from a single textbook or from state- and district-mandated curricula rather than from actual scholarly work or experiences gained by the teacher. The standards movement requires that students work and try to learn individually because that is how they are going to be tested: as individuals on norm-referenced, pencil-and-paper examina-tions. No meaningful assessment of collaborative efforts and success is utilized. What is deemed meaningful in schools is becoming more and more dependent upon the power brokers who now dominate schooling in the United States: politicians and other noneducators who have their own reasons for keeping down the children of the underclasses.

Surely, one would assume, our schools teach problem solving. Well, yes and no. I once taught "critical thinking" to sixth graders. In my course, problem solving was one of the main foci and, as luck would have it, I had the students working in groups most of the time. I say "luck" because I was not yet aware of the importance that industry placed on collaborative problem solving; I just believed that my students behaved better when working together and it seemed that the product of their work was of higher quality. So, yes, schools do teach some problem solving, or at least intend to, as evidenced in the stated learning outcomes of the various state curricula. But are students really learning to problem solve in real-life, pragmatic situations? Not according to what I read in the standards; there is little connection to the students' lives, especially if the students are underprivileged. When problem solving as well as other critical thinking skills are introduced in classrooms, they are to be learned individually. As noted earlier, the literature on global workforce skills tells us that workers will need to solve problems in a team setting, a strategy of the quality movement that energized U.S. industry in the late 1980s and '90s and motivated them to become competitive with the Japanese. How can our students solve problems in cooperation and collaboration with their peers (and teachers) if they must expend so much energy preparing for individualized exams? And still, most teachers rely on teacher-centered classrooms and teaching strategies where students are not encouraged or even allowed to work together. Cooperative learning is referred to as "cooperative cheating" by many traditional teachers.

Technological learning may be the strength of U.S. schools in regards to the four areas of workforce competencies. Our schools have invested millions of dollars in technology in the past two decades, not only in student learning but also in the daily operation of their organization. Still, teachers claim that they are not adequately trained to stay ahead or even keep up with the students' knowledge of technology. (The Swedes, however, had such advanced technology in their classrooms that it seemed as if I were at NASA!) Those of us who are parents understand young people's adeptness at using computers. The most startling aspect of technology education is the gross lack of it in many urban and rural schools, as mentioned previously. These schools lack the funding to keep up with the rapid advancement of computer technology, and even more harmful, the students coming into these schools are more likely than students in suburban schools to not have access to this technology at home.

Then there are the entrepreneurial competencies of risk taking and creativity. American schools, as a rule, thwart the advancement of both. Granted, we have art classes and music classes, but often these are rigidly structured and monitored; even when they are not, they at least exist within a rigidly structured school organization. Band students still must adhere to the "bell schedule" that causes students to respond mindlessly to the sound of the bell, moving like cattle in crowded hallways. Do students use creativity in the core academic classes of English, social studies, math, and science? The standards movement tells the teacher and the students exactly what is to be learned and when. How creative can one be in that environment? Risk taking is and always has been discouraged. The primary function of schools has been to control students; ever since compulsory education reached high school–aged children, increased graduation rates became a goal, and classrooms became overcrowded. I devote an entire chapter to power and control, but suffice it to say, our schooling as it is currently structured and operated has no room for risk takers, be they students, teachers, or administrators.

These four workforce competencies (or skills or qualities or traits) are what some forward-thinking individuals inside and outside the business community propose schools should foster in *some* students. I believe business would like us to develop only certain students into knowledge workers who will succeed in the global economy. Too often, I have worked with teachers who teach classes in a "co-op" program that allows students to gain credit going to school in the morning and working in the community in the afternoon. The objectives of such programs are supposed to be the gaining of workforce skills for the students and promoting partnerships between schools and the business community. Unfortunately, the schools' partners are usually fast-food and retail businesses that require their workers to be on time, follow directives of superiors (including the unseen superiors who write the company policies and "vision"), and be able to perform mundane, repetitive tasks. Sound familiar? Yes, the companies are looking for second-wave, industrial-age workers, those who do not think but are subservient to higher powers. What type of student opts for such programs? It should be no surprise that few are college bound and most, I would venture to say, come from low SES homes. These students are being relegated to working a string of dead-end service jobs, an ugly by-product of the global economy. The four competencies discussed earlier are for those who want to succeed in the global economy, not just subsist. What we have is a divisive message from industry: train your best for the global economy, but send us the others so they can be lowly paid sheep in our fastest-growing sector of the economy: the low-wage, few-benefits, and no-job-security service industry.

To foster knowledge workers in the global economy, we strive for these global workforce competencies. As one of schooling's clients, industry in the global economy must have its needs met as best as possible, and perhaps these needs do include having an endless supply of second-wave workers for the service and retail sectors. Yet, the primary client of schooling is the student. And what is in the best interest of the child? Is it to keep low-SES students working in the service industry while ensuring that the higher-SES students are capable of competing and succeeding in the global economy? To keep down the low-SES students, we merely need to stay the course of the standards movement whose intent seems to be the enforcement of mind-numbing curricula followed by rigid, punitive testing. Many politicians as well as educators would prefer the latter for reasons of power and control. Teachers and administrators are in great fear of the "underclasses" and the threat of violence that they pose. So are the politicians, whose shortsightedness and perhaps prejudiced actions have created this underclass whose existence they blame on educators—and they give schooling the obligation of fixing the problem, or at least pacifying the poor. Schools continue to be, and they have been for at least a century, great sorters of social classes. Ironically, conservatives rant about the liberal agenda of social engineering when that is exactly what the traditional school model promotes: social engineering to ensure that the poor remain economically as well as politically impotent.

These powerful allies—neoconservatives and neoliberals alike—have as their main concern the keeping of the social status quo through the use of mind-controlling values rather than workforce skills. Neoconservatives, however, wish to return schooling's function to merely teaching basic knowledge, the type of knowledge that ensures that people are kept in the second wave of civilization. This knowledge is affectionately and effectively called the three R's: reading, writing, and arithmetic. Granted, if one cannot read and write, he or she is not going to function well in our society. But we need to move far beyond these basics if we are to succeed in the global age. This move requires a vast change in the way we conduct schooling, the death of industrial-age schooling, and the birth of schooling for the global age.

Another, maybe cynical, view of neoconservatives' intent is to privat-ize schooling so that their religion of choice can operate a parochial school at the expense of all taxpayers. Vouchers, as I noted earlier, often are not valuable enough to allow a poor child to attend a private school; however, if a child is already in a private school, then the $3,000 or whatever the voucher is worth could be deducted from the tuition paid by that child's parents. This, of course, is public support of religion and, although the legal battles have been and are being waged concerning separation of church and state issues and although the early results of studies are nebulous concerning vouchers' ability to improve schooling, it appears that vouchers are not going away any time soon. The $3,000 used by the parents to send their child to a private parochial school is $3,000 taken away from public schools. Any way you look at it, this only widens the chasm between the haves and the have-nots.

In short, we enact laws to send our children to school (or be schooled at home) so that they can be prepared to live and work in our society. Unfortunately, our rural and urban schools are funded to function only as warehouses, keeping children off the streets and out of the workforce as long as possible. Schools also function as great social sorters to ensure that those coming from a certain social class will remain in that class. Schooling for social sorting and warehousing children is not very expen-sive as compared to schooling for success in the global age, at least ini-tially. More resources will need to be given to those who need it the most; that is the idea behind equity, which is the central theme to state school-funding models. Unfortunately, politicians from wealthy areas have a great deal more influence than those whose constituents are in poverty; and the higher the level of politician, the more likely he or she will be influenced by the wealthy. Despite efforts in equity that would mean more money for schools in need, the wealthiest children continue to have the most educational resources. As ugly as it may sound, we have a system of schooling in the United States that is not designed to adequately educate everyone, as it would be too expensive in the eyes of those who wield power. A wise man once told me that American schooling is designed with this saying in mind: Educate the best, shoot the rest.

PART II

MAJOR OBSTACLES
TO CHANGE

In part II, I examine the major problems that must be overcome so schooling can meet the challenges of the global age. First, as implied by the comments of Swedish educators after their visits to Florida schools, U.S. schools need to overcome our seemingly culturally insidious need for power and control. Global organizations must empower those within them, thus releasing centralized control. Also, deeply ingrained in our Anglo culture is individualism, a concern for schools that wish to prepare citizens to work together in global organizations and in a public democracy. I conclude part II by contrasting individualism with collectivism and describe the benefits of balancing an individualist culture with a collectivist culture within our schools.

FOUR

Power and Control

In addition to changing the structure of schools and promoting curricula for individualized learning, teaching methods in Sweden officially changed after the 1994 Education Act. Students were to be given control of their learning and, with this control, would come responsibility. The teacher's role would become that of facilitator. Both teachers and administrators were forced to become more democratic in their approach to children. This was difficult, some veteran teachers admitted to me; however, they also noted that the results were self-evident to educators. In some ways, teaching was easier in that students were more motivated to learn but, they explained, the planning of lessons was more intense. The schools I visited had very flexible class schedules that allowed large groups of elementary students to be left with little supervision and secondary students with no supervision. Because the students were serious about their work and had been "socialized" (perhaps as early as preschool), conflicts between students were rare. In fact, the two principals at one high school could remember only one physical fight in the last several years at their school of 1,200 students. Fourth-year high school students insisted that they had never seen two students fight in their fourteen-plus years of public schooling and this was in a school district with a high percentage of immigrant students or students who were sons and daughters of immigrants from a variety of cultures very unlike that of Sweden. Empowering students appears to have had positive results in Swedish schools, results we can realize in our nations, as well.

After briefly outlining some of American schools' most serious problems (including violence) to a group of Swedish middle school teachers, one veteran teacher stated that his country's schools suffered from many of those problems in the past. The past, I found, was the late 1970s and early '80s, when he was a young teacher. Violence was never a problem, he conceded, but the role of the teacher and how the classrooms were structured were much like what I described in America. I asked the group if they found it difficult to change the way they ran their classrooms. Yes, a few said. One replied, "It was worth it. The students are much more prepared to learn."

After each of my visits to Swedish schools, I pondered how this type of schooling could be replicated in the United States. Other U.S. educators, who had also visited these schools, said that teaching in Sweden would practically be a dream compared with what they had to endure in America, such as controlling central offices and state departments of education. They felt that they had little autonomy in their jobs of educating children; autonomy is indeed a casualty of the accountability movement and the fatal weapon is the standards movement with its incessant testing and mandated learning outcomes (benchmarks, standards, etc.). The Swedish teachers I spoke with believed that they had significant autonomy and that, despite the existence of a national curriculum, they felt they had the power to decide what was to be taught and how it was to be taught in each classroom. Furthermore, teachers embraced and implemented the idea that students should be involved in decisions about their learning.

The "Swedish message" I took back to the United States was met with tremendous skepticism. American educators I spoke with "rallied around the flag," as we in the United States tend to do when we are critically compared to another country. In fact, many simply ended discussions with me by saying that I should just move to Sweden if I liked it so much. Still, I was haunted by the dream of actually teaching my students instead of merely marking time with them. Perhaps it is acceptable to expose our schools' or our nation's shortcomings so long as we do not hold them in an unfavorable comparison to another country. But my intentions were and are to improve American education—and if it takes swallowing our pride a bit to admit that there might be a better model, then so be it. True patriotism is accepting criticism for what it is worth so that it can be used to improve our nation, our people, and our schools. Why should Swedish children receive an education relevant to the global age while ours are forced to learn mundane facts, facts that they will only regurgitate onto a test and then forget, while enduring an oppressive school environment that is determined to simply control children? Our children also deserve schooling for the global age; one could say it is our patriotic duty.

CONTROL IN U.S. SCHOOLS

Control and the perceived need to control are the main obstacles that American schools must overcome if we are to establish schooling for the global age. The group of Swedish visitors concluded, after only two days of visits to Florida schools, that control is the overarching theme in our education system. Teachers control students, principals control both teachers and students, central offices control everyone at the schools, and the states control all of education through high-stakes testing that both punishes and bribes through the use of ill-conceived accountability weapons. I had experienced no other way until I had gone to Sweden. My colleagues who dismissed the stories of my Swedish experiences also knew no other way. Control is ingrained into the minds and routines of American educators. Unless we have experienced a different model, it is extremely difficult for us to accept any other way.

I begin my examination of control in schools by going into "the trenches," that is, the classroom level. Teachers are confronted with large numbers of children in their classrooms, numbers that tend to make learning difficult. As a middle school teacher, I sometimes "taught" as many as 180 students each and every day. Just learning their names was a daunting task, let alone ensuring that they were taught anything. With thirty-five to forty students in each classroom, teachers who use traditional teaching methods see themselves as outnumbered and horribly overwhelmed.

As the traditional teacher I once was, I felt that I had to somehow establish an environment where I was in charge, in complete control. That meant that no one spoke while I was speaking. In fact, no one spoke at all unless that person raised his or her hand and was called upon at my discretion. This type of power was what made me feel comfortable—for a while, anyway; otherwise, I would feel physically intimidated by the sheer number of students who faced me each and every class period. Wielding power over the students gave me the control that traditional teaching methods in traditional classrooms necessitated. It was "me against them."

Besides the need for feeling physically safe, I knew that the other teachers expected me to be in control. As both a teacher and an administrator, I never heard a teacher say that his or her colleague was a good teacher because the students *learned* in that class. The definition of "good" was based on control. Why is Ms. Jones a good teacher? Because she has control; she doesn't take any crap from the kids. How do other teachers know if another teacher is in control? It surely is not because they have witnessed that teacher in the classroom because teachers have a tendency to close their doors when the bell rings so as to work in isolation. Teachers learn of other teachers' performance through hearsay only, from students' offhand remarks and from hallway and teacher-lounge rumors. I did not want to be the fodder for such rumors. Soon, however, I found that the bulk of my classroom time was spent controlling children and not helping them learn.

In about my fourth year of teaching, I was reintroduced to "cooperative learning," where each student takes a role in a small group and the product of the group is to be collaborative. I say "reintroduced" because as an undergraduate student I was exposed to this strategy but was advised by veteran teachers my first year to "forget all the crap" I learned in college about teaching. After an interesting training session on how to make cooperative learning work, I decided to give it a try. I took to it very seriously and planned its implementation quite extensively, but my students did not know how to act because they were accustomed to learning independent of their peers. Learning together, after all, was cheating according to traditionalists. Eventually, my students grew accustomed to cooperative learning, and I was able to use it two or three days a week. From what I could tell by their on-task behavior and the quality of their work, they learned better this way. Two problems, however, manifested themselves: noise and administration.

Noise was a concern of the teachers who were around my room. One year, I had only a folding wall between me and another teacher. Her class was very traditional, very much controlled. And very quiet. Despite my attempts to keep students' voices discernible at a distance of only three feet (I actually went around to each group with a yardstick reminding them that they should only be heard as far as a yard away), my classes were indeed noisy. But the students were engaged in learning, so why should I be concerned about noise? I must have gained some notoriety because a professor from the local university began sending her students to my classroom to observe collaborative learning. When these college students appeared at my door, I immediately escorted them to different groups, encouraging them to engage with the students in their learning. This, of course, only increased the noise level. I enjoyed having visitors (I was working at a professional development school, yet nearly all my colleagues used the "skill and drill" approach to learning, which makes me wonder how much professional development was really taking place) and relished opportunities to discuss the learning environment of my classroom and the collaborative strategies that I used. People from the university seemed to appreciate this, but those at my school did not. I had to constantly apologize to the teachers around me for my noisy classroom and the fact that groups of students were learning in the hallways (I hesitate to say students were "working" when they are learning, as I have found that given the right strategies and environment, learning is fun, not work). Students did not belong in the hallway; that is what classrooms were for, I was reminded. I suppose my colleagues' reasoning was that learning could not take place unless students were sitting upright in desks aligned in rows.

Most important, however, I had to convince administrators that what I was doing was effective. After first implementing cooperative learning, the administrator who was to conduct my annual assessment came into my room, looked around at all the students in groups, then at me as I busily moved from one group to the next, and told me that she would return when I was "teaching." I took no offense as I understood that the state-adopted assessment instrument that she was to use could not easily assess any teacher except those who taught traditionally—the storied "stand and deliver" type who is the only active being in the room. I eventually had to put on a dog-and-pony show for my administrator, ensuring that she was able to see everything that the ineffectual instrument asked her to see. When she left, my students asked if we could go back to the way the class was before. Of course, we could and we did.

Teaching in this manner caused me to relinquish a great amount of control. I had to trust that students would learn without coercion. Traditional approaches to teaching ensure that the teacher does not have to rely on trusting students. The threat of severe punishment and a rigid environment keeps students controlled. Trust is irrelevant. By the teacher "not smiling until Christmas," the students know that their teacher is not their friend but their enemy. This is a harsh statement, but if you worked with someone who never smiled at you or anyone else, would you not think this person was against you? At least you would believe this person to be miserable. Many teachers are. The adverse conditions (rigid bureaucracies) under which teachers work is the most cited reason for teachers leaving the field, more than lack of pay and prestige (Ingersoll 2002). No wonder many teachers are miserable and do not smile until Christmas—or ever.

⚹ SCHOOL STRUCTURE AND CONTROL

How a school is structured is a result of several factors, all of which are beyond the control of the teacher, at least in the traditional school. The two most important factors that make schools and school systems (and classrooms, for that matter) organized in a bureaucratic fashion are lack of external competition and a traditional mind-set. Schools are essentially organized in the same way as they were at the turn of the twentieth century. A principal sits at the top of the hierarchical school pyramid with one to as many as nine assistant principals a level below him or her (the number of assistants depends on the size of the school, the seriousness of the discipline problems, or the ability of the principal to convince the school board that he or she needs the support). Assistant or vice principals are even divided into layers of bureaucracy in some large schools. In two assistant principal jobs I had, I was to report to another assistant principal (AP) before I could see the principal. These higher-level APs are usually in charge of curriculum or administration. This usually means that the curriculum AP develops the master schedule for students and teachers and the administration AP supervises facilities and sometimes athletics. In some sports-crazed school systems, the position of athletic director is given administrative power, and may even hold the same power as the principal (or more). At one school where I was an AP, the school's design had the principal's and athletic director's offices side by side, identically designed. In a move to show respect for academics, the principal eventually (and wisely) placed the athletic director elsewhere.

In cases where APs are divided into different levels, the ones at the bottom are what were formerly known as "deans." This is most typical in large middle and high schools. These are the people to whom students must go when they are discipline concerns, at least in the teacher's estimation. Based on my three years of experience in this position, this might be the worst job in all of education. Practically every decision this AP makes will either upset a student, a parent, or a teacher, and every decision has the potential to be overturned by a higher-ranking AP, the principal, or someone in the district office if the parent has political connections in the community. In one innovative district where I was an AP, administrative assistants were hired to work the primary student discipline problems. APs were left to deal with curriculum and administrative concerns. These administrative assistants usually did not have or need a college degree, and they did an excellent job working with students and parents. APs, in most cases, are required to have a master's degree, usually in leadership. I could never understand what my master's degree in leadership did to help me to deal with children in conflict and their parents. Perhaps, if one possessed a dual major in psychology and criminology, with an emphasis in crime scene investigation, then his or her schooling might be applicable. When the Swedish principal and superintendent visited my school, which had six administrative assistants, they could not contain their wonder as to why a school would need six adults to work full time on disciplinary issues. The way we conducted schooling was the answer.

"Below" the APs are generally the team leaders in elementary and middle schools and the department chairs in the high schools. Administrative assistants, when used, are somewhere below teachers, not because of their lack of importance, but because of their lack of formal education. Team leaders are those who are designated by the principals as the contact person for a grade level or other combination of teachers in an elementary school, and an interdisciplinary group of teachers in the middle school, where four or five teachers teach a different subject but share the same group of students. Team leader or department chair meetings are held regularly so that an administrator, usually the principal, can dispense orders from his or her office or from the district office (memorandums and e-mails apparently do not have the same impact as a face-to-face meeting with the school's leader). Information trickles down to the other teachers through the team leader or department chair. This requires regularly scheduled meetings for the teams and the departments. Department meetings rarely result in anything more than a regurgitation of information handed down from administration and resulting complaints about administration. Sometimes, however, discussion occurs regarding curriculum: what teachers are going to be allowed to teach or what curriculum mandates are at each level. These discussions are usually moot points because they are easily resolved by rereading the mandated state and district curriculum guidelines. Rarely do meetings involve personnel from more than two layers of the bureaucracy. When they do, it is such a large gathering that no one is allowed to express a concern or an idea. By allowing only two layers to meet at a time, delineation of power and control is maintained.

Up to this point, I have discussed three or four layers of bureaucracy at a large school in an attempt to allow the reader to understand the formal power structure of such a school, but I have not yet reached the bottom where the least powerful reside. Teachers are at the next—but not last—level of the pyramid and they understandably feel disempowered by their lowly status in the structure. With several layers of positions above them, their ideas rarely make it to the principal and are therefore rarely implemented, assuming the principal even has the power to implement the idea. But teachers need not feel totally impotent, for they can still use the classroom as a place to dominate the students who are bottom-dwellers of the pyramid. (To save the reader from sheer boredom, I have omitted the description of other layers, such as guidance counselors, social workers, school psychologists, career specialists, school resource officers, teacher aides, custodians, groundskeepers, cafeteria managers and workers, bus drivers, and perhaps the most powerful of all in a school building, the secretaries whose influence with administration and ability to expedite or slow down the paper shuffle give them unparalled strength in the schools.)

Students are indeed at the bottom of this huge bureaucratic structure that is called a school, and the even larger structure that is the school district. Students can be thought of as automobile chassis that are placed onto the assembly line of schooling and, over twelve or thirteen years, gain added value as would a car going through an assembly line, or simply tossed out somewhere along the line, labeled as rejects. What comes out after high school graduation is a completed model, at least that is the intent. American "models" of students coming off the line are as outdated as the Edsel and maybe as relevant to the global age as a Roman chariot.

Students have no power. Most schools have student councils that discuss such mundane topics as the theme for the homecoming dance or the preparation of French fries in the cafeteria. In contrast, I witnessed a student council meeting in a Swedish elementary school where the principal valiantly steered the conversation away from such inane topics and on to how the school is governed and what is important to be learned. Some U.S. schools, mostly high schools, allow student representatives to sit in on the school improvement team that also consists of parents and teachers but is always dominated by administrators. The decisions they are allowed to make are about as unimportant as those that the student council makes.

A concerted effort has been made across the country by school officials and by politicians at all levels to give more control of schools to parents—or at least allow them to be heard. Being allowed to express one's views and having one's ideas implemented are separate issues, but parents can and do sometimes garner control of schools. In a Florida school district where I was an administrator, a group of parents guided by the Christian Coalition decided to do something about the "godless" schools in our district. They campaigned fiercely to get two of the coalition's members elected to the school board. Considering that the board only had five members and one member was already overly sympathetic to the coalition's cause, the fate of the schools was in this right-wing organization's powers. The first item on their agenda was to institute a Bible study class in all eight of the high schools. Of course, this violated federal law, but a well-known televangelist assured the school board that his organization would pay all legal fees. This was the largest school district (50,000 students) that had attempted the initiation of such classes. After hundreds of thousands of dollars spent on legal fees, the two coalition members were rendered powerless on the school board and were eventually replaced by citizens less inclined to religious zealotry. This is merely an example of what level of power parents, and community members, can have on schools when that power is left unchecked by professional educators.

A positive example of parental power is the willingness to fight the bureaucracy. Usually I commend parents for their tenaciousness to defend their children and what they believe is right. Dress codes, for the most part, are silly and a serious waste of teachers' and administrators' time. When I witness parents who fight against these codes, I give them my moral support. I would never have said publicly, when working in a school, that parents were right in fighting these codes, as this would have been political suicide for a young administrator whose chances of advancement rested more heavily on political connections than on job performance.

Parents do, however, abuse their community position occasionally, as exemplified by the Bible curriculum fiasco in Florida. Often, they will simply bypass the school level and call the superintendent directly. Of course, they almost never get past his or her secretary because the superintendent's secretary is uncanny at being able to deflect or defuse conflict—as is the principal's secretary. When deflection is used, it is a deflection back to the school level, which has orders to "make the problem go away."

Of course, wealthy or politically connected parents can get an audience with the superintendent and even school board members, the latter being a better choice for the parents. School board members do not want any controversy because they depend on every single vote. School board elections, after all, attract only about 5 to 10 percent of registered voters. School board members also tend to be very protective of their job, despite its often part-time status. In Florida, where school districts are countywide, the school board member is a very powerful person politically, as school boards are often the largest employer in the county. A parent cannot go wrong by gaining an audience with a school board member. Something will always be done to rectify the perceived problem at the school in question or at least the parent will be pacified in some way. Parental power is definitely at its most potent when it is used at the top of the school bureaucracy: electing school boards or helping appoint superintendents. The movements to ensure parental input in day-to-day activities at the school level are ineffective due to the ability of school officials to deftly deflect outside opinions, merely appeasing parents by allowing their participation in impotent parent-teacher organizations.

Despite my alluding to the power held by school boards, I have yet to describe the power hierarchy at the district level. Beyond the principal are various administrators who hold both de facto and de jure power in the district. Depending upon the size of the district (I was employed by school districts ranging from 35,000 to 175,000 students), a central office may consist of only a few layers of bureaucracy or as many as several dozen. In large districts, the principal has a direct supervisor who, in turn, reports directly to an assistant superintendent, who, in turn, reports to the superintendent—unless there is another level in between, that of deputy superintendent or some other concocted title. Curriculum supervisors abound in district offices, and although they may have quite large support staffs, their power is miniscule relative to the administrators above the school principal.

In times of delirious stress while an AP, I thought of diagramming a portion of the district's hierarchical pyramid on one of my office walls. At the bottom would be an arrow pointing to me and the words "You are here." Then red arrows would point to every stop along the way the parent must go in order to get his or her opinion heard. I imagined each administrator's business card in a holder fastened next to that person's place on the wall. This way the parent could (1) see the futility in fighting the system (unless that parent had the political clout to go straight to a school board member), and (2) if the parent decided to embark on this journey, at least he or she would know the players. A picture next to each administrator's name would have been a nice touch—that way the parent might get the opportunity to confront him or her at a grocery store!

Again, at the bottom of the pile is the student. We educators are reminded at nearly every district or school training session that our job revolves around the children, yet the children have no voice, no power. They simply ride through the assembly line called schooling, hopefully having value added at each stop. When they are released from this assembly line, they are expected to be active participants in a democracy.

Newly graduated teenagers have not been educated to participate in a democracy, nor have they even been exposed to a democracy. Traditional schooling is a near-perfect example of an autocracy. Students experience an impotent life at the bottom of the bureaucratic pyramid of school. They are to strictly adhere to rules made by adults who exist on higher levels of the pyramid and, if they choose to challenge these rules, they are severely punished. Traditionalists argue that children and adolescents are not capable of making decisions, and to some degree they are right. But if decision making were nurtured in our youth so that they could learn to make informed decisions about their lives and their communities, then the traditionalists' argument would be nullified. As our schools are now structured, one of the crucial elements of real democracy, questioning authority, is stymied by the authoritarian structure and the culture that is built around that structure, a culture of distrust of youth and a resulting emphasis on control.

FEAR AND THE
OVEREMPHASIS ON CONTROL

Schools in the United States have been tightening control for decades due to a myriad of factors, most notably cases of horrid violence exemplified by the Columbine High School tragedy. It is now common for schools to have security guards in the hallways and to meet any visitors, who most likely have been funneled into one highly secured entrance. In addition, random checks for both weapons and drugs are commonplace, as is the use of metal detectors. School violence is a real concern but, according to some studies, it has actually been on the decline in the past decade (NCES 2000). School violence only seems to be on the rise due to its coverage by the various media. Other control measures actually began prior to the spate of media coverage of school violence. School structures, policies, and punishments have restricted actions and, perhaps, the rights of students. I contend that the increase of controlling measures and the condescending attitudes of adults within and outside schools are due to the continuing lack of respect for authority.

Questioning authority is a necessity for a citizen in a democracy, although knowing how and when to question authority is a skill that must be gained by our students. School officials speak often about the erosion

of respect for teachers and other school officials over the past generation. Of course, every generation, dating back at least to the ancient
Greeks, has complained about the lack of respect it receives from the
youngest generation. I do believe that America's school officials have a
legitimate concern, and it does not surprise me at all that students have
much less respect for authority than previous generations have had.

My own theory is that this lack of respect began as a reaction to the
Vietnam War. Children in the 1960s, such as I, grew up seeing the flaws
of our federal government. Although I was inundated by patriotic stories and songs in my elementary school (a brainwashing that is perfectly
acceptable in this country), I could not help but wonder why so many
young people opposed the military's actions in Southeast Asia and was
numbed by the bloody war scenes on the nightly television news broad-
casts. In 1974, when the Watergate fiasco came to our attention, junior
high students began to truly question the motives of the highest authority in our nation; I know because I was among them. Watergate also
unleashed the media on our politicians and other notable people. (A
history professor of mine once pointed out that although Babe Ruth was
at times a drunken whoremonger, the media ignored it. Yet, when it
was found out that Kansas City Royals third baseman George Brett had
hemorrhoids removed between games in the 1980 World Series, every
time he ran out to his position, the television cameras "zoomed in" on
his backside.) The "gentlemen's agreement" not to cover certain aspects
of a person's life became null and void by the mid-1970s.

Next came the constant barrage of criticism toward Jimmy Carter and
his handling of the economy and the hostages in Iran, followed in the
1980s by the Iran-Contra mess, and the savings and loan cover-up that
seems now to be forgotten. The myriad of scandals that hit the Clinton
White House, most notably the Lewinsky affair, made authority even
more suspect in the eyes of a new generation. The Roman Catholic
Church is embroiled in controversy regarding sexual molestation by
priests. The corporate scandals of Enron, Tyco, and Global Crossing,
among others, will hopefully cause our youth to question where and
with whom they place their money, plus question the unbridled support
all levels of government give to corporate interests. As of this writing,
we are engaged in a globally unpopular military campaign in Iraq, which
may only lessen authority's esteem with our children as well as the rest

of the world. This weakening of authority at its highest levels has a "trickle-down" effect, an effect that reaches the schools as well as the family. Whether or not justified, this questioning of authority is now engrained in our society.

It is no wonder that school officials report that they receive less and less respect from students. The actions of our highest officials and the coverage given them by the media have tarnished the images of politicians and those in power, and the cost is a reduction in respect for teachers and administrators. The reactions by schools are to tighten the control of students through more rules and stricter punishments. One example is the "zero tolerance" movement in response to violence and drug use in schools. Gone are appropriate actions to help the students understand the repercussions of drug use and of harming others. In their place are swift, rigid actions taken against students, actions such as immediate suspensions, expulsion, alternative schools that resemble prisons in function and purpose, and arrest leading to incarceration in both juvenile and adult facilities. These overreactions greatly hinder schools' efforts to create trusting, democratic learning environments in which students become responsible citizens. Trust is replaced with constant supervisory vigilance by adults, such as teachers, administrators, security guards, and police officers housed at the schools. In addition, security cameras are commonplace in schools everywhere, be they urban, suburban, or rural schools. While some students and most parents feel better about this added security, the students cannot help but feel that they are not trusted.

We know from management studies that the more someone is supervised, the more that person needs to be supervised. What we have created are cultures of control and distrust. As control increases, trust decreases. As trust decreases, so does responsibility. We are damaging our children and the future of our nation by the support of school "prisons." A more reasonable way to attack the problem of school violence is to seek and attack the core of the problem. Why are students being bullied? (Bullied students are often the culprits of school violence in acts of retaliation.) Instead of answering this question, schools and school districts establish zero tolerance policies toward bullying. This causes more students to report bullying, which is good if it is warranted, but it also causes adults to resolve conflicts that are better resolved by children. We could, as adults, provide the victim of bullying with strategies to deal with bullying or mediate between the bully and victim (better yet if the mediation is conducted by other students). Instead, we severely punish the bully without determining why the bully took his or her actions, nor do we attempt to determine why the victim is indeed a victim.

As with our reaction to the crisis identified (or manufactured, depending on your perspective) by *A Nation at Risk*, we have chosen to simply "do more of the same" in regards to school violence: more rules, stricter and swifter punishment. And, as with the school reforms of the past two decades, our tightening of control on schools has had negative effects on both our children and our society. We are still viewing ourselves and our children as sheep that are to be controlled. Most of us in schools, unfortunately, are playing the part of shepherd quite well—or maybe the role of wolf—just as most of us adults unwittingly play the part of sheep in our society. We follow the media cues so as to mindlessly sleepwalk through life, not having to concern ourselves with the ugliness of society, the ugliness that schooling for the global age can help to alleviate.

FIVE

Balancing Collectivism and Individualism

When I asked a Swedish couple how their seven-year-old son was progressing in his first year of compulsory education, I was told, "Okay, I guess." This seemingly uncaring answer was startling to me, considering the boy's mother was a teacher and his father a high school principal. His mother went on to say that if anything were wrong his teachers would inform them. Reading my puzzled look, she went on to explain that Swedish schools concentrate on social skills at an early age, not academics. According to the results of recent international comparisons (NCES 1999) and from my own studies in Sweden, this approach seems to be working. By the time Swedish children reach adolescence, they perform better than students from most developed nations, including the United States.

The Swedish National Curricula promote collaboration and democracy in the classroom and throughout each school. Competition and individualism are discouraged. The Swedish society has long been known for promoting the good of the group over that of the individual. One ancient Swedish saying is that no blade of grass should stick out higher than another. Modesty is a virtue, as is helping your fellow human being to succeed. This is in stark contrast to the American "rugged individual" who would be considered weak if he sought another's help (especially government assistance). It is also our heritage to "look out for number one" and then, if one has the resources, to be condescendingly charitable to others. In order to develop global-age schooling, we must temper our penchant for individualism and foster a desire to work with and help others.

75

TRUST, INDIVIDUALISM,
AND HERO WORSHIP

Collectivism, the promotion of the group's needs over the needs of the individual, is embraced throughout much of the world. This is contrary to the individualist culture that is dominant in the United States, where we celebrate the individual over one who compromises and sacrifices for the good of the many. In fact, to compromise is sometimes seen as weak and even treacherous. We are, after all, the nation of the first person singular: me, myself, and I. Our heroes are those who are not willing to compromise, who "stick to their guns" no matter what the odds. We believe that our hero, who is independent from others' needs and seeks only to promote himself, will lead us to a better place, a better nation. Our folklore is full of such individualist figures as Daniel Boone, the lone pioneer, to fictitious characters like Paul Bunyan and John Wayne (the characters he portrayed on film were not as large in our collective psyches as the image created by the actor John Wayne). We still seek to find such heroes in our sports figures and politicians, yet the inquiring media keep us from fully embracing many of these people due to revelations of their personal habits, as noted in chapter 4.

If we are to promote more teamwork and collaborative learning, we must disregard much of our folklore and develop new stories to tell our children about great figures in history who worked for the benefit of the many in a peaceful, collaborative way. America does indeed have such people who were often also martyrs for their cause; unfortunately, these people do not make good subjects for action-type films and books. Martin Luther King, Jr., and Abraham Lincoln are two famous examples, yet they did not physically defeat other men in fistfights nor lead men into combat against evil regimes. Therefore, they do not fit our need for rugged individual action heroes; they were mild-mannered, caring, deep thinkers who, although greatly admired, do not fit the mold of the great American hero.

A large contributor to our inability to work well with others is due to the type of hero we worship. This certain hero is deeply rooted in our Anglo-American heritage and will not easily be replaced. The cowboy is a perfect example of this type. He (not she) was a rugged individual who stood for virtue, only interacting with others, it seemed, when he was

needed to single-handedly subdue evil. Of course, this figure is mythical; we have no people in our past who actually were like this. John
Wayne, who personified this cowboy hero, was not really a cowboy, despite what we would like to believe (hence, his image being used recently to sell beer). Although he only played cowboy heroes in his films,
he went to great extremes to cultivate an image as a rugged individual
hero. Kirk Douglas once detailed in *Parade Magazine* about a time in
the 1950s when Wayne approached him after a screening of *Lust for
Life,* a film in which Douglas portrayed the artist Vincent van Gogh.
Wayne asked Douglas why he would play such a person, implying that
Van Gogh was hardly the typical American hero. Douglas explained that
he was an actor and that was his role; he was not really Van Gogh nor
was he any of the characters he had played in previous films. John
Wayne implied that Douglas should only be playing rugged individuals
whom our society would glorify. Douglas could not help but be amazed
that John Wayne actually thought he was indeed John Wayne, the character who saved numerous Western towns from bad guys dressed in
black, and the character who had almost single-handedly won World
War II in film after film.

To this day, we worship these rugged individual types. I dare say most
of Ronald Reagan's popularity was due to the image he developed as
a self-made pulled-himself-up-by-his-bootstraps success story. What a
contrast he was to the introverted Jimmy Carter and the quiet, serious
Walter Mondale. America wanted a hero as a leader and instead they
got an actor who played heroes in film; this seemed to satisfy most of
us, as Reagan's approval ratings were consistently high throughout his
eight years in office. George H. W. Bush was more hero-like than Michael Dukakis, the former having been a World War II combat veteran.
Yet his demeanor was not like that of a hero; the nation had been duped,
or so it seemed. The backlash against Bush caused the nation to embrace a pulled-himself-up-by-his-bootstraps little-known governor from
Arkansas. But he had fooled the nation, also. He was, of all things, an
intellectual!

Intellectuals, according to stereotype, cannot be heroes because they
are weak in physique as well as in convictions. We demand someone
who says what he believes and sticks to it, even if the belief has no evidence to support it. This opened the doors for George W. Bush. Al-

though he did not win the popular vote, he was and is embraced by most Americans, especially after the terrorist attacks of September 11, 2001. To his credit, he successfully cultivated the image of American hero: a tough, down-to-earth cowboy despite being raised in an aristocratic environment. Even though he attended both Harvard and Yale, he has never portrayed himself as an intellectual. He is the cowboy hero our culture craves, or at least he plays a cowboy in front of the television cameras. And this he did when he made his way to ground zero in New York City to proclaim to America and the world that he would make the terrorists pay. America loves Bush's "rootin' tootin'" image that simplifies the world for us—that is, good guys (who are us) and the bad guys (who are not like us or at least not *with* us)—thus, the "Coalition of the Willing." We finally have the hero we have been lacking since Reagan.

I would like to use President Bush for "hero dissection," as he is an almost perfect example of the cowboy hero. What is it about him that we love and seemingly need? First of all, he appears to be an "everyman." He uses simple language and appears not to quite comprehend the complicated world around him, as evidenced by his lack of world political and geographical knowledge in the 2000 presidential campaign. Bush used simple tactics and spoke simple phrases to win over the American people. In times of crises, we will "rally around the flag," that is, we become very patriotic and look toward our president to fuel this patriotism. President Bush does not let us down. He wrapped the flag around himself after the 2001 terrorist attacks and again in the war with Iraq—and we loved it, at least according to the president's approval ratings. Because he talks tough against those who disagree with us—or worse, those who want us dead—we feel safe with this cowboy in charge. Our penchant for heroes has given us exactly what we crave: a cowboy who will stop at nothing to prove his point—even, some would say, alienating most of the world and destabilizing global order to do this. Heroes, we believe, should stick to their convictions and, for better or worse, this is what Mr. Bush does.

Individualist societies, such as ours, look for a hero to lead them to a better place, at least as long as that person does not try to change our American ideology. The basic values of life, liberty, and the pursuit of happiness, as worded by Thomas Jefferson, find their origins in the writings of John Locke, who advocated individualism as well as democracy.

Locke opposed a strong central government for fear that it might empower the poor, whom he deemed incapable of making the important decisions necessary to drive a nation. Jefferson believed in a "public democracy" as described by David Sehr in *Education for Public Democracy* (1997), one in which everyone has the opportunity to influence our nation's future.

Jefferson probably never intended for nonwhites or women to be included as "everyone." Jefferson desired a democracy that would promote a meritocracy where those (white males) who were blessed with a desire for hard work and possessed high intelligence would rise to serve the people, acting in their behalf based on their voiced needs and desires. In contrast, our nation adopted a private democracy where it seems that participation is limited and elected officials represent the needs and desires of the powerful and wealthy, those who were instrumental in getting them into office.

In this private democracy, each individual's right to accumulate wealth exceeds the rights of the society as a whole—thus the belief that governments should be weak, not interfering with the individual's desires. Yet, our federal government continues to usurp power from the individual states, growing to the point that it has a tremendous hold on all of us. Even with this "hold," we Americans still believe that we are in control of our lives, that we are free to buy what we want, live and work where we want, not bothered too much by government. Conservatives would like even more freedom from government; they strongly feel that individual Americans should have as much freedom as possible to seek the American dream of life, liberty, and the pursuit of happiness. This can only be accomplished, according to conservative doctrine, by creating strong individuals who neither seek nor need help from others—especially government (yet family connections and the preferential treatment accorded to a white male are perfectly acceptable).

The conservative doctrine of individualism continues to dominate our government as well as our society at all levels. Living the lie that we are free, we feel compelled to force our way of life upon others in the world. Our "freedom" lies only in our ability to buy whatever we can afford (or not afford, due to "predatory lending"). We are not free to truly influence the politicians who make policy and the omnipotent multinational companies that practically own the politicians and our government.

Public democracy supported by global schooling would benefit us by (1) giving power to everyone by fostering the desire to participate and the knowledge of important political issues, and (2) leading us away from our individualistic nature to support issues that are for the good of everyone in our society, a society that also includes everyone who lives in the global village.

An irony of conservative thought is that it is based on a belief that we are unable to be trusted with our base desires without having rigid laws and customs to control us. We want to think that we have freedom, but—without going into the depth of politics that many other books have covered—many of those freedoms are being eroded. In education, teachers seem to either believe all children are inherently good or evil. Often, teachers refer to having "bad kids" who must be strictly controlled or permanently removed from their classes. This desire to rid themselves of "bad kids" led to state laws that allow teachers to have certain students taken out of their classes and off their class rolls if the students are judged by the teacher to be disruptive. From my experiences, relatively few teachers actually try to use these laws, as the alternative to having an unruly student in their class is to place that student in one of their colleague's classes. No one deals with the reasons the students are disruptive in the first place, which may be linked to their schooling being disconnected to their lives and irrelevant to the world around them.

How does this belief that people are born evil affect our desire for individualism? One of the differences in conservative thought and liberal thought is what happens once someone has failed or succeeded. Conservatives, in general, take the strong individualist stance that anyone who has failed has done so on his or her own, through poor choices, or is simply genetically inclined to fail. Liberals tend to believe that the person has failed in part due to problems with society, such as racism or sexism. Conservatives say our nation's individualist ideology is perfect; therefore, the foundation upon which this nation was built has no flaws. Anyone who fails must look inside himself and, of course, find a way to "pull himself up by his bootstraps." It is not government's responsibility to correct an individual's error or shortcomings. Liberals, in contrast, generally believe that the imperfect society that has developed over the past few hundred years in America is the primary reason for people's failures or successes; therefore, they promote government help for individuals needing it. Although, in theory, liberals would seem to favor individualism because they strongly believe in the self-regulating abilities of all of us, they seek a collectivist means to correct the imperfections of our society, especially those that cause us to fail. Those who succeed (and by "succeed" and "fail," I am referring to the American scale of material wealth) have done so by their own "pluck" and other favorable characteristics, according to conservatives.

The fact that the overwhelming majority of successful people are white Anglo-Saxons only proves (in the eyes of conservatives) that the Puritan work ethic really works. This simplistic thought, this enormous lie, has allowed individualism to flourish in our nation. I think it safe to say that the vast majority of conservatives are of white Anglo-Saxon descent (or wish they were). If they can make it in America, why can't everyone else? When liberals speak of social injustices and other flaws in our society, conservatives tend to perceive it as an attack on the successes and values of the white race, especially white males, because the Anglo culture is paternalistic.

Our nation was built on the belief that one can consistently improve oneself through hard work and good decisions: the Puritan work ethic. By abstaining from evil habits and deeds, one can reach the fullest extent of *his* potential (women and minorities are not included, as they were believed to be inferior and should only hold supportive roles in our society). Our heroes personify the Puritan work ethic and dutifully follow laws unless they believe them not to be righteous. These nonrighteous laws were, of course, installed by weaker, compromising men who did not work their way to the top of their profession but swindled others along the way to the top. Therefore, it is the duty of the hero to break these laws. The duty for the rest of us is to (1) follow our heroes, (2) obediently abide by others' rules (unless a hero has shown us that we should not), and (3) distrust anyone who does not personify, at least in part, the rugged individual. This belief system has allowed generations of white men to improve themselves economically—at least until this past generation, when for the first time in U.S. history a generation cannot expect to do as well as the one before it.

It is at this time in history that we must seek different heroes, disperse different folklore about truly great Americans; we must search for heroes and folklore that establish that those who seek the good of the group are superior to those who "go it alone," selfishly finding ways to improve only themselves. At a time when top executives of multinational companies steal from their workers to make obscene personal financial gains, the need for different heroes is crucial. By continuing to promote the rugged individual as hero, our children will not be prepared to work and live in third-wave organizations and in an ever-changing multicultural global society, and our schools will continue to be nothing but irrelevant industrial-age relics. We very well could be left out of global-age success. The end of the age of America may soon be upon us.

ALL FOR ONE, ONE FOR ALL

Sweden has a collectivist society, but it is, of course, not the only one in the world—just the one with which I am most familiar. Although Sweden is a small country, its economic successes are quite impressive. But Sweden is not the only country to have such success, and other countries may be more readily compared to America, particularly Japan. Japanese industry was able to easily implement W. Edwards Deming's quality principles, in part because the Japanese people, and thus the Japanese workers, embraced the concept of working toward a common good. It is also understandable why American industrialists would not attempt to introduce such a concept in the few decades following World War II because of our learned hatred of the Soviets and other communist nations. The Japanese did listen to Deming's ideas, believed in them, and implemented them. They also reaped the benefits of quality management and organizations, unlike Americans who continued to rely on extrinsic incentives (e.g., salary increases). Of course, U.S. industry finally realized in the late 1970s and early '80s that they, too, needed to increase the quality in their products by ensuring quality in their organization and their management—yet, they encountered resistance, both from management and from labor. For too long, supervisors supervised and laborers labored, each dependent upon the other. This led to a culture of distrust that negatively affected the climate of the workplace and, ultimately, the products and services provided.

The auto industry is often used as an example of a successful transformation toward quality. The "big four" automakers in the United States (General Motors, Ford, Chrysler, and American Motors) had lost much of their American market share to the Japanese and, to a lesser extent, the Europeans. Ford Motor Company called on Deming, who laid the foundation for quality in that company, but warned of the need to have patience. U.S. companies are notorious for their concern with the "here and now," the profit statement for the next quarter. Other U.S. automakers followed Ford's lead and began to copy the Japanese experience with quality, especially in the formation of work teams. They soon found that it was difficult to institute these teams due to a management style that sought to control and a workforce that only knew how to work under direct supervision, coercive tactics, and ever-increasing extrinsic rewards. By changing the management style—which would, in turn, change the motivation methods employed—the American worker could become more self-reliant and, eventually, autonomous. An autonomous worker needs no supervision; companies save money by decreasing or eliminating middle management, and profits soar—in theory. This scenario, I honestly believe, is already being played out in American industry. Collectivist structures and cultures are proving to be successful in American industry; they would be even more successful if U.S. managers and laborers were more collaborative in nature rather than competing against each other, both at different levels in the organizations and within the same level.

Anthropologists refer to collectivist societies as "allocentric" and individualist societies as "idiocentric." In the latter, self-efficiency and achievement are valued; in allocentric societies, people depend more on each other for support and to accomplish tasks. If being able to effectively work in collaboration with others is a quality necessary for success in the global economy, it would seem that those workers with allocentric cultural backgrounds (most Asian, African, and Latin cultures) would be at an advantage. Being able to work in a team setting is one of the most important, if not *the* most important, quality for the global workforce. Are Anglo-American workers at a disadvantage due to their heritage of idiocentricity?

At present, the answer to that question would be "no," considering the dominance of the Anglo culture in the United States, but as other global regions begin to compete at an equal level and perhaps surpass the United States in economic might, this could change. The European Union, if it can continue to remain strong while expanding eastward, has the resources and the educated workforce to overtake the United States. Further behind but with even more potential are the Pacific Rim nations, led by Japan, China, Taiwan, Singapore, and Indonesia. Their tremendous combined population and allocentric societies make them a formidable competitor in the world market. But in order to participate in the global economic theater, a nation or region's economy must be large, at least as large as the United States, which is currently the most powerful force in the world economy. To play with the "big boys," one must also become big. The Europeans understand this and will soon equal or surpass the United States, especially if the United States continues its current trend of deficit spending. The potential for an Asian coalition, one that might include India, is overwhelming to consider. They are even more prone to be collectivist in nature, especially in the workplace.

JAPAN AND THE RISE OF
A COLLECTIVIST ECONOMY

Despite the current economic woes of the Japanese, I believe we can learn much from their successes over the past few generations. It must be noted that Japan's current economic problems are due mostly to a shoddy banking system, not poor management. The Total Quality Management principles that were outlined by Deming in post–World War II Japan are still effective and help ensure that the productivity level of the Japanese worker remains very high. Without this tremendous productivity, the Japanese economy would most likely be in a free fall.

One important reason for TQM's success in Japan was that the Japanese were willing to delay gratification, something that is seriously lacking in the American culture. Deming warned the Japanese that they would not meet with success until after at least a generation. American businesses find it difficult to agree to such a plan that would not ensure economic success quickly. Even though many American industrial organizations were "on the ropes" in the late 1970s and early '80s and needed to change the way they conducted business in order to survive, I still find it hard to believe that they were willing to consider TQM because of this necessity to delay gratification. (I am not convinced they ever did completely embrace this concept. Major corporations are still too focused on short-term profit.) The Swedes and other allocentrist societies accept delayed gratification to a much better degree than we, mostly due to their traditions of collectivism.

In order for workers to accept the vision of a chief executive officer (a vision that has hopefully been shared, not forced), they will likely want to know how it benefits them—in the short term. That is something from which our workforce must be weaned, and this can be initiated in the schools. Educators can do more to promote long-range goals for students versus daily grading and feedback demanded by the bureaucratic system, distrust of parents, and the lingering hold behaviorism has on schools and teachers. As a teacher, I found that I could appease parents by providing weekly progress reports; as an administrator, I met with parents who demanded daily reports from teachers regarding their children's progress and behavior—even for eighteen-year-old "children"! This desire for constant feedback can be attributed to parents not trusting the teachers to do their jobs or their own children to be doing what they should be doing—that is, learning.

Quality control in industrial-age organizations requires constant checks on products rather than TQM's insistence that by establishing a quality process and environment, quality of product and service is inevitable. Parents who know nothing but second-wave organizations, especially schools, expect constant feedback on their children. As teachers, we are deluged with behaviorist theory as undergrads, convincing us that we can modify students' behaviors so that they will do anything and learn anything as long as the right stimuli are provided. In some ways, this belief keeps us from leaving the profession. If we did not embrace the idea that our actions, and those of the parents, can have a direct effect upon the student, then we would be attributing all student success to genetics. By continuing to provide constant checks and feedback of students, however, we are fostering instant gratification. We do the same with our workforce. By making some sacrifices today, they can see by the vision that they share with management that they will be rewarded later. One such sacrifice is the discarding of the individualist

attitude, a seemingly insurmountable hindrance to TQM and all global-
age organizations.

AFRICAN AMERICAN COLLECTIVISM
AND SOCIAL JUSTICE

In discussing African American's collectivist society, it must be noted
that urban schools that are predominantly black maintain overly controlling environments, the antithesis of the global organization. Both black
and white teachers use more directives with African American students
and establish authoritarian classrooms. Sadly, the black community accepts and expects this. The consensus among urban educators, including those at the university level, is that teachers must be more direct
with black students; they cannot allow them choices. For example, a
black child will supposedly believe that the teacher does not care about
him or her if the teacher is not constantly and firmly ordering the child
to work. A teacher in a predominantly middle-class white school might
say to a student, "You should put down that Gameboy and finish your
reading." The expectation is that the student will indeed place the toy
in a book bag and get back to studying. The argument of urban educators is that if you say that to a black child, he or she will understand that
statement as simply a choice. The word "should" implies that the student really does not have to comply. The teacher must say to the African
American student, "Put down that Gameboy and finish your reading,"
leaving no doubt as to the intentions of the teacher. It can be argued
that the tonality of the teacher should be firmer with the black child
than with the white child. Research conducted in urban settings has
suggested that this is the best way to get black students to comply with
authority (e.g., Wilson and Corbett 2001; Delpit 1995; Weiner 1993; Irvine 1991). Therein lies the problem.

Do we want an entire culture to be dependent on authority's demands? The global worker and citizen must be capable of autonomy,
working without supervision and willingly participating in the democratic social processes. If the research is indeed accurate, then why is it
African American students demand directives from authority figures?
The answer may be deeply rooted in culture, a culture still affected by

the legacy of slavery. White authority had for centuries demanded—with threats of brutal physical punishment—that black slaves do the tedious and arduous work that was seen unfit for the white man or woman. That has had a profound effect on the culture, but it does not explain why it still exists 140 years after the Emancipation Proclamation. The explanation, I contend, is what blacks have endured in these past 140 years of African American "freedom."

De jure and de facto discrimination have been the norm for the African Americans since slavery was abolished. In the South, Jim Crow laws relegated blacks to the underclass, subservient to whites. It was the same in the North, only more deviously implemented because laws were not actually on the books, yet social mores demanded black subservience. What are the effects of these discriminatory practices of subjugating blacks to menial employment, if any employment at all, and to brutal public treatment? Because I am not black, I cannot speak for African Americans, but I strongly believe if I were black that I would not be inclined to trust authority of any kind. I would not desire to do work that seemingly has no meaning to me or my future, especially if it were simply *suggested* that I do it. It would indeed take a strong directive to get me to perform these meaningless tasks. Student activity in the industrial-age school is often meaningless. What connection can the black child make in performing mundane activities to his or her world, especially if the activities are linked to a curriculum formed by whites for whites?

Cultural relevancy—that is, connecting black students' learning to their lives—is an important movement in urban schooling. It is significant in the learning of every student, regardless of race, but with American blacks, who have been oppressed for 400 years, it is crucial. But beyond the connections made to children's lives, how can black students know that success in school is correlated to success in life, especially in the age of globalization, if they have no proof? Most urban and rural black children live in communities where education and income levels are extremely low, and therefore no models exist for connection between academic success and success in life. Instead, the media provide a constant barrage of role models from the entertainment field, and these are too often negative (athletes and other entertainers who live

lavish lives of self-indulgence and a live-for-today, self-gratifying existence).

If one does not believe that those in authority are to be trusted, then
one certainly would not abide by their suggestions to work, especially if
that work were meaningless. The need for directives has been embed-
ded into the black culture through four centuries of mistreatment and
understandable mistrust of white authority (or black authority, if a black
person is acting as a tool of whites). So let us return to the perception
that black students require directives in order to engage in learning. If
we first examine the actual learning that is to be taking place (that is,
examine it through the lens of cultural relevancy), we take the correct
initial step to resolving this problem. Second, we must establish for
blacks that success in school really will allow them to find the material
success that they see in the media, the so-called American Dream. (I
am not a proponent of material success as a measure of success in life,
but it may suffice for this argument.) In order to establish the connection between schooling and material success, we must critically examine
the curricula and "learning" methods forced upon urban schools.

FORCING INDUSTRIAL-AGE SCHOOLING
ONTO AFRICAN AMERICANS

Urban school curricula are essentially skill-based, intellectually demoti-
vating, and reeking of the industrial age. The preferred method of in-
struction is "skill, drill, and kill" in that students are expected to repeti-
tively perform mundane tasks until they know the nonsensical
knowledge "dead." Teachers bark out information and directives, and
students memorize just long enough to pass their low-level proficiency-
type examinations (the aforementioned "bulimic learning"). These
exams assure the public that those leaving high schools have the rudimentary, second-wave learning that they themselves gained from their
schooling, appeasing many neoconservatives. It also ensures that neoliberals will have the underclass they need to perform the menial, low-
wage service jobs that our economy is wont to create. In other words,
keep African Americans in subservient positions in our economy and
our society. In order not to appear accusative by saying that there is a

conspiracy among some to keep blacks "in their place," I will just say that this type of schooling does indeed keep blacks at the bottom rungs of the economic ladder, whether it is the intention of the powerful elite or not.

John Ogbu (2003) conducted studies in suburban communities and found that middle-class blacks do not perform as well as their white counterparts. Controlling for SES, his studies suggest that something is amiss in the African American culture that keeps black students from succeeding—perhaps the remnants of slavery and Jim Crow (by law or by fact) and the mismatch between schooling and material success. In a study conducted two decades ago, anthropologist Jay MacLeod (1995) followed two groups of poverty-class, urban high school–age boys. Mac-Leod found that one group (mostly African American) believed in the concept that school would be the catalyst to success, taking them out of their hardscrabble existence into the middle class. The other group (mostly white) rarely attended school; instead, they abused drugs and alcohol throughout the days and nights. Depressingly, eight years later, MacLeod returned to his study site only to find that just one of the boys from either group had found material success. This was the only white teenager in the black group, and he was "succeeding" through the peddling of illegal materials. The group of young white men was about where one would expect: in prison or languishing in poverty. Surprisingly, the young black men who attended classes regularly, did what they were told to do by the teachers, and embraced the message that a high school education would lead to material success, were no better off than their substance-abusing white counterparts. Reality struck them harshly. Their schooling was not relevant to material success; they were not able to overcome a background of poverty by learning their high school curricula.

MacLeod's findings should have been the beginning of the end for industrial-age schooling; instead, they were and are ignored by most educators. We, middle class Americans (including most public school educators), want to believe that what we do makes a difference. Most of what we do does not, I am sad to say. By embracing the "get tough" standards movement with its proficiency tests, bribing and threatening schools and students, enticing parents to abandon public schools so that all of schooling can be privatized (further widening the gap between rich and poor, whites and nonwhites), Americans are "shooting them-selves in the foot," ensuring their demise as an economic power. Worse yet, we are perpetuating social unrest by rendering people of color pow-erless. This social unrest cannot be contained forever; we can only build so many prisons and hire so many police, especially if we also intend to be protectors of the world and cleansers of all regimes deemed "evil" by our leaders. High-tech militaries are expensive to maintain.

Returning to African American culture and collectivism, how can we use this tendency of blacks to work for the good of the group to help them succeed in school and life? Somehow, we must extinguish this seeming need to give and take directives. Cultural relevancy may help to motivate some black students to learn, but the manner in which they are schooled must change. If we as educators continue to foster this dependency upon directives in futile attempts to force children of color to learn instead of nurturing decision-making skills through the use of choices, then we are only exacerbating the ever-widening achievement gap between blacks and whites, both in and out of school. The Japanese found Deming's ideas workable, in part, because their culture was col-lectivist; the same can be said of the Swede's acceptance of progressive education, as it is noncompetitive and promotes collaboration among learners. If blacks are allowed to embrace their collectivist roots, learn-ing in environments that are cooperative, perhaps they can experience academic success and, thus, empowerment. And if the mainstream white society does not begin to embrace the collectivist-oriented pro-gressive schooling models, then it will not only be surpassed by the Pa-cific Rim and European regions, it will be surpassed by black society if blacks continue to be segregated and utilize progressive global school-ing. This could very well allow for urban blacks to be freed from sepa-rate but inferior schooling, into which they have always been subju-gated, into separate but superior schools. By ensuring that all students—black, white, Hispanic, Asian, or any ethnic or racial persua-sion—learn in global-age schools, then our entire society (that is, the United States) can remain economically powerful. And almost as impor-tant, we will be able to stand morally upright and respected by the rest of the world.

SELLING COLLECTIVISM TO
THOSE IN POWER

Advocating for a more collectivist culture as a means to promote social justice will only be "preaching to the choir," in that those who will listen are already believers in the importance of social justice. The way to ensure that collectivist values become widespread in our society, thus promoting social justice and high educational achievements for all, is to convert those who are in control of education's future. By establishing the fact that collectivism can increase worker productivity and subsequently benefit industry, many people might gradually embrace the type of schooling that this book promotes. Connecting collectivism with long-held values, the values upon which this nation was founded, might bring some leaders over to global schooling ideas. I want to first build the case for collectivism increasing worker productivity.

Global-age organizations require a considerable amount of collaboration through teaming and other structures. This is because organizations of the future (and of today) require great flexibility to meet the ever-changing needs and desires of consumers. Flexibility cannot be achieved by top-down management. Flatter organizations consisting of various teams of collaborative workers enable companies to adapt to their environments and remain successful. In order for workers to successfully collaborate, they require not only good interpersonal skills but also the ability to solve problems within groups of workers. Of course, our schools are still industrial-age relics that require students to learn individually. By restructuring schools into flat, team-oriented organizations that promote students to work and learn collaboratively, students will be prepared to thrive in the global economy.

Adolescents leaving our K–12 system of schooling greatly lack the abilities to work with others; instead, they are competitive for grades and position. Competition was introduced in schools as a way to motivate learners and to prepare them for the "real world." It did, indeed, motivate some to learn, and it might have prepared them for the workforce that once existed. Some are indeed motivated by competition, and the minority that does succeed in a competitive environment has historically been well rewarded by society. Their success in school might be due to a greater propensity for industrial-age learning—that is, rigid, forced memorization and regurgitation. To be successful outside school, they needed to be and were the beneficiaries of a certain class, race, and gender. But what about the vast majority who did not "win" at school? Before the middle of the last century, most Americans did not graduate from high school and only a handful out of every hundred students entering public schools could expect to earn a college degree. This was not a major concern at the time, as the industrial age was in full swing in the United States and anyone could get a well-paying job if he (note that gender; being white is also implied) simply possessed the Puritan work ethic.

At least this was true by the 1950s, because of the great accomplishments of the labor movement, the devastation of the rest of the industrialized world, and the lack of industrialization of the Third World. There was no need for Americans, at least the white majority, to embrace a cooperative nature. The "cowboy hero" of American lore had done quite well to establish the most powerful nation on Earth. But at what cost? The cost is an ever-widening gap between the haves and the have-nots, and between whites and minority races. Left unchecked, this gap will widen to the point that both sides will either violently collide or simply slide into the abyss.

ESTABLISHING COLLECTIVISM
AS AN ATTAINABLE GOAL

My plan for educating youth for the global age calls for collectivism to at least balance out the individualist tendencies of U.S. society. Those who control public education are typically both politically conservative and embrace individualism. How can we convince these forces that collectivism is essential without making them believe that schools are promoting socialism, communism, or some other "un-American" ideal? This can be accomplished by embarking on a campaign of democracy and "flying the flag" around the notion that every one of us is a strong individual with the capability to make a difference. We cannot fixate on the collectivist part of schooling for the global age or else we run the risk of having this restructuring squashed, but instead we must promote the values aspects of the global-age curricula. All school leaders, administrations, boards, and state personnel support schools in promoting values—as long as they are agreed-upon values.

Democracy, responsibility, and trust are seemingly benign (in the sense that few would debate their worth) yet powerful values. What politician, no matter on which side of the congressional aisle he or she sits, can argue with fostering democracy in our schools? This, most of us believe, is what our nation stands for. In a truly democratic nation, all become equally empowered. A first step is for leaders to see that schools are promoting democracy, which we all love, honor, and cherish. (I am being only partially facetious in that I am somewhat fearful of advocating empowerment of the oppressed in this time of American nationalism spurred by globalization and the current administration.)

Responsibility is another value that is universally endorsed. I frequently hear teachers and parents complain about children not taking enough responsibility for their actions. Individualism does require this, but collectivism does even more so. By promoting global schools to foster responsibility in students, the same responsibility that was evident in Sweden, then all constituents should be pleased. Employers should be ecstatic to have a workforce that is responsible for its own individual actions. Of course, with this responsibility would come a high level of learning because students would be required to formulate their own learning plans and follow through with them. Global organizations require such a responsible worker.

What about the system of service-oriented businesses that employ our disadvantaged, the ones that keep them in virtual poverty? If our students become too responsible and learn too much, who will work for these companies? Hopefully, the need for such workers will greatly decrease in a globalized economy. A highly educated, responsible workforce can only increase the value of any company and the economy as a whole. Workers who are capable and not afraid to take risks and demonstrate high levels of creativity are the entrepreneurs that all companies need in the global economy. I just hope that the employers do not become too shortsighted, as American business executives are wont to do.

Others—chiefly neoconservatives—should embrace responsibility because it is one of the core values that they strive to institute in schools. The Puritan work ethic that fundamental Christians promote so heavily calls for one to be responsible for his or her own actions, akin to individualism. Schools cannot do wrong in fostering the value of responsibility in children.

Trust may be more difficult. Of course, we all believe that it is important to trust (especially politicians whom we do not know) and to trust everyone that we know well—that is, those who are close to us. How could anyone argue with the fostering of trust in our children? Well, perhaps organizations that embrace industrial-age management will not want to trust workers because they are seen to be full of flaws, a belief that humankind is inherently evil; therefore, the organization must constantly control these evil beings to ensure that they do well. Industrial-age management styles have never trusted workers. Those employers and managers who are more intellectually evolved, who embrace TQM and other global-age management styles, will understand the need to trust and be trusted. (This is difficult to write considering the recent fleecing of America by executives at Enron, Tyco, Global Crossing, and so forth. Businesses want to trust employees but employees may find it impossible to trust the executives who hold most of the power. It might take a long time to reestablish a workable level of trust between employees and employers in large companies.)

What about the neoconservatives? Fundamentalists, I would imagine, would want to be able to trust their neighbor so that they do not have to build even higher fences and more sophisticated security systems. Hopefully, they want to be able to trust Catholics, Jews, Hindus, and (maybe someday) Muslims. The problem is indeed "fundamental": how can we trust someone who has been offered salvation through Jesus Christ but has refused to be "born again"? Surely, these "nonbelievers" cannot be trusted by some neoconservatives. They must be closely watched until the Rapture. I overdramatize, of course, and I sincerely hope I am misrepresenting their way of thinking. The fundamental religious zealots in all parts of the world are the most opposed to the blending of cultures and races in the global era. We need to find some way to sell the concept of trust to all constituents, perhaps by linking it so closely to responsibility, which it is anyway, that no one will be able to refute it. I, for one, believe it can be accomplished.

PART III

A NEW MODEL FOR THE GLOBAL AGE AND BEYOND

Chapter 6 presents a schooling model for the United States that emphasizes values over academics in curriculum, practice, and structure. The successes of Swedish schooling that I have chronicled throughout this book are due in part to their willingness to postpone an academic focus until they are sure their students have the foundation required to be democratic citizens. I propose the three core values that I came away with from Sweden as well as "openness" (inviting real community participation) as the pillars of this curriculum, and then proceed to explain the new roles each stakeholder of our schools must play and the new goals of the schools in order for this new model of schooling to succeed. Many of the ideas presented in this new model are explained in further detail in chapter 7, which is essentially a vision of schooling for the global age. In that chapter, I revisit the core values and other aspects of the global school model and connect them with the global community, ending the chapter with a key to global school success: early childhood education, something to which our nation has paid too little attention. Chapter 8 describes the organizational change necessary for global schooling to proliferate, directly addressing the obstacles first described in part II. Finally, chapter 9 covers our moral obligation to prepare all our children to succeed in the global age.

Six

A New Model of Schooling for a New Era

On my last trip to Sweden, I spent time collecting data on how three schools in one community supported the Swedish National Curricula. (The Swedes have adopted curricula at three levels: one for high school and adult education, one for seven- through fifteen-year-olds, and one for preschool.) The major foci of these curricula are democratic learning environments; trust among teachers, students, administration and, to some extent, the community; and the responsibility given and accepted by students. In addition, I found that their schooling model, especially at the high school level, promotes what I refer to as "global workforce competence" (teamwork, problem solving, pragmatic technological skills, and entrepreneurship), as described in chapter 5.

The Swedish National Curricula are value-laden documents that are not based on academic standards; they are vision statements of what schooling should look like and what type of person this schooling should foster. These curricula are passed down from the Skolverket (National Department of Education) to each of the 278 municipalities, which choose how to implement the values stated in the curricula. The schools take the municipality's implementation plans and mold them to their own needs. In turn, teams of teachers, then each individual teacher with the help of his or her students, continue to shape the curricula to meet their own needs. (Other documents, referred to as "syllabuses," actually contain a few vague academic standards. I found that most teachers disregarded the syllabi, except those who prepare ninth-grade students for the one and only mandatory national examination that they must pass in order to leave compulsory education. Nationwide, 98 percent of the students pass this exam.)

The Swedish Education Act of 1994 and the ESEA of 2001 mandated by President George W. Bush are both examples of federalization of education. The difference is in their implementation and in their vision: the ESEA is a mandate based on past assumptions of schooling success (without respect to whether those assumptions are accurate). The Swedish federalization of schools, on the other hand, allows each municipality to mold the plan to fit its needs and the vision of the act was for the future, the global age. It is based upon values, whereas the ESEA's base is high-stakes testing. The ESEA gained bipartisan support in Washington due, in part, to the nation's distrust of schools.

Most citizens seem convinced that our schools are failing, or at least lagging behind other nation's schools—and I agree, with qualifications. Our schools are at least lagging, if not actually failing—but not because we are no longer concentrating on the "Three Rs," and not because we no longer stress obedience, punctuality, and repetitive and mundane student tasks. We are indeed teaching the "Three Rs" in the schools; in fact, the schools are stressing these "skills" to the point that other— perhaps more important—skills are ignored. The perceived educational needs of the political forces behind school reform in the United States are naive, insufficient, misguided, or even diabolical. The global economy requires much more than these traditional skills produced by schooling. Unless one hopes to be nothing more than a minimum-wage, underemployed service worker, then the latter view is actually a hindrance to a person's entrance into the global workforce. No one would ever say that reading, writing, and mathematics skills are not important—they simply are not nearly enough for success in the global economy. Our students could learn them much faster if they were motivated to learn. Increased motivation requires schooling to be much different from the industrial-age schooling you and I received, and which our students still receive today. It must be relevant to the global age, fostering an understanding and a desire for democracy in every child.

Although I am a proponent of national guidelines for education, I do not agree with the logic behind the ESEA mandates. These are written for the industrial age and are punitive in nature. Truly effective national guidelines would meet the core of our nation's and world's problems: social issues. Our economic woes are not caused by a workforce that cannot read and write. They are a result of globalization of the world's economy and our belated attempts to engage in this globalization. Re-member, it took at least a decade of losing economic ground to the Japa-nese, Germans, and other Western economies for U.S. industry to real-ize that their management style and organizational structures were at the root of their problems. National educational guidelines should pro-mote global workers who can work collaboratively in a team setting and not perpetuate the industrial-age assumption that they are in cutthroat competition with all others in their company. Guidelines should also promote problem solving in collaborative settings—problem solving for situations that exist and situations that could arise (proactive managerial approaches). Understanding not only how to use state-of-the-art tech-nology but also understanding its benefits and its effects upon industry and society are crucial for education in the global age. Finally, promot-ing risk taking and creativity so that students can be prepared to exist and succeed in a volatile and too-often uncaring economic environment would be essential objectives of effective federal education guidelines for preparing students for the global workforce.

Preparing students for the workforce is not the only or even the most important educational goal. The core problems within this nation and internationally do not stem from economic concerns, but social ones. For instance, racism is a ticking time bomb waiting to explode in our society. As schools become resegregated because of inequitable state funding and the continued segregation of housing, racism festers in our collective wounds. I am deeply concerned for the well-being of those who are left behind in stark, understaffed, and underfunded urban schools. I am equally worried about what control devices the majority race will implement to "keep minorities in their place" at the bottom of the economic ladder. Educating them for the industrial age or for pov-erty-persistent service jobs—as is the result (and possibly the intent) of the ESEA/No Child Left Behind mandates—will only exacerbate the race problem.

So what can schools do to ensure that students are prepared socially to combat social ills? UNESCO (United Nations Education, Social, and Cultural Organization) has a laudable plan for the world's schools that the United States should study. Regardless of any administration's polit-ical views toward the United Nations, we as educators need to learn from those who have an effective, holistic vision for the global village, such as UNESCO.

In the mid 1990s, UNESCO proposed that schooling should focus on what they call the "four pillars of learning" (Delors 1998). The first pillar is *learning to know*, which is much more than rote memorization; its intent is for students to gain a deeper understanding of content. *Learning to do* is the second pillar and is something that few standardized tests can measure, and that traditional schooling does not promote. John Dewey championed experiential learning nearly a century ago, yet has been largely ignored ever since. Another aspect of learning promoted by UNESCO is *learning to live together*. The Swedes focus their early education programs on this skill. Why be concerned that a student is behind in reading, writing, or math skills when that student cannot function in society? We are social beings who, first and foremost, must get along with others. The major concern of teachers, year in and year out, is not their low salaries, but working conditions due, in part, to the students' behavior. If our schools concentrated on teaching students to get along with one another, perhaps these behavior concerns would lessen to the point they are in Sweden: teachers could not even comprehend student misbehavior being a major concern.

The fourth pillar of UNESCO's plan is one that is quite abstract and might only be attainable in the immediate future by very wealthy nations, perhaps some of the economically prosperous countries that are not quite as socioeconomically diverse as the United States. That pillar is *learning to be*. This is a nearly existential plane of learning that I can only describe in terms of Abraham Maslow's theory of need (1987). Maslow contended that we must pass upward through different levels of a pyramid that represents our feelings of security. The lowest level is sheer survival, having not to be concerned with being physically harmed or obtaining enough to eat as well as having decent shelter in which to live. Far too many people in Third and Fourth World[1] nations are stuck at this level; perhaps most of the world's population exists here. Without dissecting Maslow's theory and subsequently each of the levels, I want to explain the highest level of security or need—the level of self-actual-

1. Fourth World: Nations forcefully incorporated into states, which maintain a distinct political culture but are internationally unrecognized.

ization, for which UNESCO argues we all must strive. This is essentially the learning-to-be pillar in that one has the autonomy to make one's own decisions without concern for creature comforts. At this level, one is not mired in thoughts of oneself but has a great feeling of camaraderie and responsibility toward others. I agree that this is a goal toward which we must strive, and that it would be quite beneficial in the development of a public democracy; however, I would be ecstatic for American children to simply learn to live together peacefully. Three out of four pillars, for the time being, would be a good start.

THE NEED FOR CORE VALUES

In order to structure schooling so that children learn to live together, we should consider the three values I sought to explore in Swedish schools: trust, responsibility, and democracy in the learning environments. I offer these as the three core values for our national curricula, values that are essential if we are to move from the industrial age and promote a public democracy for the sake of all in the global village.

First, the value of trust is not compatible with a competitive environment. I am not advocating that our nation give up on capitalism, which is dependent (maybe too much so) on competition between and among rival organizations. It is simply something that does not need to be emphasized or used in the schools. Our society fosters competition to the point where there is no need for it to be learned in our schools. Instead of focusing on ourselves as individuals and everyone else as our competition that must be defeated, we must instead focus on increasing trust among students and teachers in our schools. Trust can also be increased through a restructuring of the school organization that allows for decisions to be shared by all stakeholders in the education community, beginning with the children. Students feel that school is something that is done to them, not for them, which is understandable given their place at the bottom of the bureaucratic pyramid. Our visions of students as mere chassis being moved along the assembly line of schooling dehumanizes our children so that they have no reason to trust those who place them on the line, adding pieces and parts onto them.

This same uncaring bureaucratic system alienates teachers from authority, including administrators at the school and central office levels, as well as political authority beginning at the school board and continuing on through the state levels to Washington, D.C. The unionization of teachers is due to the mistreatment of this autocratic system that does not value teachers as autonomous professionals, but instead lays blame on them while dictating what they are to do. I had a literature professor who once said that he did not want to teach in the public schools for the same reason he did not want to work in a factory. Why would you want to go to college only to have a job where you come home to your wife each evening complaining about the foreman? The foreman treats the factory worker with disdain, supervising the worker's every move because that worker, it is believed, cannot be trusted to do the job without coercion or the threat of it. Administrators and politicians feel compelled to control teachers in the same manner due to their lack of trust of teachers. They apparently feel teachers cannot be trusted to perform their job assignments without constant supervision and stifling mandates from above. Yet, we are discussing educated people, college graduates. That is exactly how work life is for many (if not most) teachers in our schooling system. They are not trusted by their "superiors," so they, in turn, do not trust the students.

Lack of trust for schooling exists at a higher, broader level—our whole society. We as a people do not trust schools to educate our children. This is apparent in national surveys (e.g., Rose and Gallup 2002), although it is interesting that a person's local school is deemed better than the nation's schools in general. The media play a crucial role in this lack of trust, but so do schools themselves. Television, radio, and the print media are watched, listened to, or read only if they have something interesting for the audience—thus, their penchant for negative sensationalism.

After a bomb threat and evacuation of 3,600 students in a school at which I worked, a television crew questioned a colleague of mine wanting to know who was responsible and how the perpetrators were going to be punished. (Our society loves seeing others punished!) My colleague turned the questions around, asking why the crew was not there the day before when 1,500 students were being honored for high academic achievement, but arrived at breakneck speed to report on some student calling in a phony bomb threat.

As studies indicate (e.g., NCES 2000), school violence is down over the past decade but media attention to school violence has increased over 400 percent during that same period. Sensational stories, or at least stories that are reported as sensational, are part of what keeps society from trusting schools. Schools, in fact, are doing a better job at doing what they are designed to do than ever before in America's history. Educators give a basic education to a higher percentage of the population than at any other time in our history. The problem is that this basic education is for the industrial age, which helps to explain why society's lack of trust of schools is partly schooling's fault. If we educators were cognizant of the new wave of civilization, we would have changed schooling so that it would be relevant to the world around us and, perhaps, we would not be the targets of current ill-conceived school reforms.

Students, for the most part, are not motivated to learn, or at least learn the content that is forced upon them in our schools. All children want to learn; otherwise, when left to their own devices, they would simply sit and stare at a wall all day. This is hardly the case; when students are given "free time," they become very rambunctious—most likely due to their actions and thinking being stifled by the system to the point that they do not know how to act without controls. By acting out and attempting to socialize, both deterrents to traditional schooling, students are demonstrating a desire to learn something, even if it is only learning how to be recognized and favored by their peers. I believe that somehow students comprehend that what is going on in the schools has little, if any, relevance to their lives and the future into which they must enter. Cultural relevancy is an important aspect of urban education, and making schooling relevant to one's culture is crucial for a person to be motivated to learn. So is making schooling relevant to one's future. We do not do that in today's schools.

Constructivist learning practices allow for individualization of learning so that each and every learner can make a connection to the curricula and his or her own individual experiences and circumstances—which are, in turn, connected to a specific culture. I have always told beginning teachers that their number one goal was to be a good role model for children because students do as they see and often not as they are told. The second goal is to motivate students to learn. Children rarely come to school internally motivated to learn content that has no connection to their lives or their future.

Responsibility, as the Swedish high school principal reminded me, depends on trust. Without responsibility, the cycle of trust is broken. Management studies suggest if workers are given autonomy in their jobs, allowed to make decisions affecting what it is they do each and every day, they will respond with high-quality, diligent, thoughtful work. Successful global organizations attempt to support trust and responsibility within their work cultures. Those organizations that have embraced quality management principles reap the benefits through higher productivity and quality work. I believe that if students are given the power to decide and develop their own learning, as I witnessed to a high degree in Sweden, then they will reward us with responsibility. I cannot explain the wonder I felt when high school students told me the reason they were in school was because it was their responsibility to learn, even after I had reminded them that teachers and administrators were not really keeping track of their attendance, a practice that is of the utmost importance in U.S. schools. We must always know where our students are because we cannot trust them if they are left unsupervised. Trust apparently was being rewarded in Sweden with responsible students who could be trusted to be responsible both in school and as citizens in a democracy.

Democracies depend on an informed and responsible citizenship. Citizens need to take the responsibility to vote and to vote responsibly: vote as informed citizens, and be knowledgeable about the issues and how they affect themselves, their community, their nation, and the world. We Americans tend to be none of these. Our democracy is therefore a private democracy, according to David Sehr (1997), one in which relatively few have power or demand that they have it. It would seem we are content to have others look after our welfare yet we voice distrust of politicians. We continue our disgruntled sheeplike behaviors because the system is devised so that most of us can do nothing but follow along; we are ignorant as to how our opinions and needs can be heard and met. Once we break this ignorance by instituting a system of schooling that fosters empowerment of all, we will force those who act as shepherds to share power. This will mark the beginning of the public democracy for which Sehr advocates. What may be the most difficult task of the formulation of a public democracy will be ensuring that the populace makes proper decisions, decisions that are based not only on each person's own needs and desires but the needs and desires of others so as to form a cohesive and compassionate society. This, in part, was the intent of Paulo Freire and, for his efforts, he was exiled from his homeland of Brazil. Promoting equity and empowerment for the historically disempowered is dangerous business.

Schools that do not embrace democracy, or cannot show the resolve to structure their organizations to become a public democracy, obviously do not model democracy to their students. As I advised beginning teachers about modeling, students do more based on what they see than on what they are told. If they spend twelve or thirteen years in an undemocratic institution, they will continue to act as if they live in an autocracy waiting to be told what to do. Our democracy, assuming we still can lay claim to one considering the apathy of our citizenry, may be turning into a de facto autocracy, where a small concentration of power controls most everyone's life. How can we expect students to participate in a democracy if our system of government remains that of a private democracy, where special interests (especially corporatists) control politicians and policy, where the citizens' opinions mean next to nothing? We now live in a nation where multinational corporations that have no allegiance to any one nation still tend to control government actions, and dictate policy and laws; it is imperative that we act quickly and decisively to foster public democracies in our schools. Children who have lived in a democracy for twelve or thirteen years will come to expect an actual democracy when they are of voting age. We will all benefit from this expectation.

Another way to ensure that children will someday expect a true democracy and exact the changes needed to establish one is through schools' use of critical pedagogy. This educational strategy and system is one that was championed by Paulo Freire in Brazil, who sought to empower the lowest socioeconomic classes of his nation to make societal changes through the use of literacy. What benefit is there in being able to read or write if you cannot play a part in your environment? Freire worked to establish literary circles of adults who, while learning to read and write, were also learning to make the changes necessary in society so that they no longer had to accept poverty as a way of life for themselves and their people. And for this, he was rewarded by being thrown out of Brazil; he went on to other nations in South America to continue his work, and eventually to Harvard and Oxford where he became an international educational celebrity. The Brazilian government, run by aristocrats, wanted to keep the lower classes down. Teaching them to read and write was one thing, empowering them through literacy was another.

We need to seriously question whether or not the powers-that-be in our nation will allow an empowerment of the masses. Using critical pedagogy to empower our students to exact necessary changes to better their stations in life may be the downfall of those who are currently in power. An Ivy League education, family connections, and the ability to work economic and political systems to one's often self-serving agenda should not be the formula for success. At this time, it is. Empowering our students through critical pedagogy can change this, if it is allowed to happen. Correlations can be made with Brazil of the 1950s and '60s not wanting their underclasses to learn and be empowered to our nation's often mind-numbingly inane curricula that emanate from the standards movement. I am not accusing the powers-that-be of trying to manipulate the educational system so that those who are historically disempowered will stay that way, but I am arguing that the schooling system that has developed and is perpetuated by mandates from Washington and the various state governments is allowing and ensuring the disempowerment of a vast number of people. If those in power have not understood this, then perhaps I am foolish to point it out. I might be nullifying any chances of instituting critical pedagogy in schools rather than the mundane skills and curricula advocated and forced upon the schools by politicians. These skills and curricula not only ensure that those who are disempowered remain so, they are also skills and curricula of an era long since past—the industrial age. Our schools must become global-age relevant in order for our society to meet with success in the global economy and in the global village.

A GLOBAL-AGE MODEL FOR SCHOOLING

What should a global-age model look like? Such a model and its curricula would stress three main areas:

- Fundamental social values
- Roles of the schools' stakeholders
- Goals of the schools and schooling systems

In this section, I describe and defend the need for these areas in a value-laden model for schooling.

Democracy

It would be difficult to find anyone in the United States who would not endorse the value of democracy, yet I wonder if we could agree on how it is to be learned in the schools, if it is at all. Some may feel that it is not schooling's responsibility to teach any values while others, such as U.S. Education Secretary Rod Paige, believe that learning values in schools is extremely important, although we might disagree as to just what those values are. Yet, in this period of time when we are experiencing rapid change in cultures, politics, and economics on a global scale, most will feel comforted by the knowledge that our students are learning some positive values, values that are deemed traditional, values such as democracy. We Americans love to say that we live in a democracy and that we are "the world's greatest democracy." The rest of the world has heard many of us say this and, in many ways, I agree with the statement. It was somewhat ironic, however, to be in Sweden in January 2001 and announce at every school I entered that I was from Florida and was there to study, among other things, democracy. The ensuing discussion would cover, among many other topics, how our electoral system counted votes and whether such a system was truly democratic.

Despite my concerns about voter apathy and politicians' manipulation of voters, I do believe the United States is still a democracy and I strongly feel that most Americans would support the fact that democracy should be taught in our schools. There are, however, different ways in which democracy may be taught as well as different definitions of democracy itself. John Dewey was adamant that students could not comprehend what a democracy is nor understand the importance of having such a form of government unless they actually experienced it. I cannot count how many times I have heard teachers say, "My classroom isn't a democracy." Some proudly state that their classroom is an autocracy or a dictatorship.

This is a vestige of the industrial age, where autocratic leaders were rewarded and revered. It may also be, however, a result of both fear and distrust of children, especially teenagers. We adults somehow feel uneasy allowing teenagers to have any power, perhaps due in part to their ability to inflict physical harm on us. I used to feel the same uneasiness. In fact, the first high school principal for whom I worked mentioned not once but three times during my employment interview that there was nothing we could do if all 1,500 students were to somehow unify and decide not to do anything we told them to do. This paranoia exists in perhaps every high school in America. And yes, giving our students power to make all decisions about their learning could be chaos, if we gave them this power without preparing them for it. My advocating for the establishment of democratic learning environments is not to immediately usurp power from teachers and administrators, but to gradually develop environments so that children and adolescents can understand what a true democracy is, how it functions, and how to actively live in one.

By emphasizing the value of democracy, we have no choice but to develop democratic learning environments where responsibility and trust can be nurtured. So the concept of democracy should be taught through the modeling of such a form of government in our schools and the type of democracy is the empowering public democracy espoused by Sehr. Considering the current state of education—mired as it is in the culture of distrust—and the differentiation of finance and power that exists in our nation, this will be a difficult feat to accomplish.

Trust

In order to foster in our children the learning of reading, math, and writing, as well as other useful skills such as basic mechanics and marketing, the school and teacher must be willing to trust the students to learn by themselves—or at least have the responsibility to direct that learning. This is contrary to our traditional mind-set about learning and schooling. We somehow have accepted as fact that children are inherently lazy and do not want to learn when, in fact, we have simply driven out the desire to learn and the curiosity that stirs such learning. Our highly structured schools with their teacher-proof curricula squash children's desires to learn. The most difficult value for the school to embrace may indeed be that of trust. Adults, through their ignorance, have learned to distrust children. This lack of trust may have its roots in our Puritan, Anglo-American background that still dominates today. Some of the first compulsory schools were built on the belief that we all need to learn to read and write so that we can extract from the Bible the necessary knowledge to keep away evil. That belief emanates from a distrust of our children and all people, a belief that if you do not control children and adults at all times, they will perform evil deeds.

A principal with whom I once worked told incoming sixth graders at our middle school that if they had to look around to see if the teacher was looking before doing something, then they probably should not be doing it. He was correct. Why do children feel compelled to do something they are not allowed to do? Perhaps, as mentioned previously in this chapter, it is because they are controlled to the point that their every action is monitored, and that when given the opportunity, they break out of the "prisons" in which we have placed them. Management theory and practice tells us that the more we supervise workers, the more they need to be supervised. When a structure is developed, such as teams, and where quality is built in, the need for supervision decreases dramatically. I thought about this often as I supervised as many as 1,000 teenagers at once in high school cafeterias. I would see students turn to see if I or one of my fellow "prison guards" was watching before they did something they knew would upset another student (e.g., throwing food). After witnessing cafeterias in Sweden where no adults were present except for the food service workers, I would ask my fellow guards (other administrators, counselors, and teachers who had drawn "the short straw" and had received cafeteria duty) what would happen if we simply walked out of the room. "Why, they would riot," was a typical reply. In fact, they might be correct, but why was this not so in Sweden? Was it because our gene pool is inferior to the Scandinavians? Of course not! It is the prisonlike structure we have developed to house our children for thirteen years, after which time we trust them to go out and participate in a democracy, making decisions about all aspects of their own and others' lives. It is ironic that we have one of the freest societies in the world (if not the most free), yet we have one of the most structured and controlled school systems. It is understandable, to some extent, that the Japanese, for instance, have highly structured school environments; their citizens live in a highly structured society because of their unique cultural norms. Yes, we are indeed the "land of the free," except in our schools. We cannot trust children because we have ensured that they cannot be trusted through the system of schooling that we perpetuate.

Responsibility

In order for a school to model democracy, the stakeholders (especially the students) must be responsible for their actions. Children are indeed children, so we can expect mistakes, lapses in their quest for responsibility. In order to lessen the likelihood of these lapses, responsibility needs to be built into each school's system. Responsibility must be fostered at the earliest possible age. For instance, a five-year-old in kindergarten would be required to develop his or her individual learning plans. (I describe Montessori schooling later in this chapter, a model that promotes responsibility, especially in the preschool years.) Of course, a typical five-year-old might not be able to do this without guidance from the teacher. The teacher, however, needs to refrain from the desire to control the situation, to simply dictate what the student is to learn. This is not easy because tradition tells the teacher to control the student, the class, and the curriculum. (Well, maybe not the curriculum since it is currently dictated by local and state governments, and indirectly, the federal government.) This is the way American schooling has been done since time immemorial. The five-year-old, full of curiosity as most children are at that age, will most likely express an interest in most any topic as long as it is active. From this interest, let us say that it is "trucks," the student with the teacher's help can build vocabulary and math skills. Starting with the word *truck*, the student can begin to understand the workings of a truck with the help of the teacher, of course, but also by looking at age-appropriate books about the topic, by surfing the Net (albeit a highly restrictive Internet access), and by dialoguing with school personnel and community members who know about trucks. This is exploratory learning and is highly motivating. I reemphasize that whatever activities the student will engage in must be active. A five-year-old (or a fourteen-year-old) is naturally active. Controlling him or her in a traditional classroom setting inhibits not only motivation but also intellectual stimulation. (I contend that if allowed to be more physically active in classroom settings, the number of children diagnosed as hyperactive or with attention-deficit disorder would plummet. It is simply unnatural to ask children, or anyone for that matter, to sit still in a highly structured environment for the periods of time we demand our children do in our schools.)

The five-year-old, by developing his or her individualized learning, is demonstrating a tremendous amount of responsibility. I understand that the topic of interest will likely change and probably often, which is perfectly acceptable as long as the student has been allowed to gain the tools and strategies for learning—if he or she has been allowed and encouraged to find resources regarding the topic of choice and has been encouraged by the teacher to learn the traditional academic areas through the topic. The nurturing of this learning strategy requires and reinforces responsibility in the learner, a trait essential in the global worker and in the global citizen.

Openness

Although openness may fall under the umbrella of trust, I believe it to be of such importance to schooling and so often absent in the schools, that I provide it with its own section. Education is everyone's business in that it does indeed take a village to raise a child; schooling, on the other hand, is traditionally the business of professional educators. Despite our current culture of distrust, professional educators must allow for more openness within their schools so as to build trust between the schools and the stakeholders. As described earlier, schools' stakeholders are many: students, teachers, parents, administrators, community members, and the business community that will employ the future graduates. American schools are beginning to open themselves to the stakeholders, at least in theory; parents and even some students are invited and even required to participate in councils with school personnel, businesses are solicited as partners for schools, and community members are sometimes invited into schools to volunteer. These are all potentially good developments for schooling and could reap some positive results. The results of allowing stakeholders to make decisions about schooling at a high level, however, are not as positive because outside forces are demanding that schooling adhere to their agendas. This is accomplished by politicians, who now dictate what schools should be like, what students should learn, and how they learn.

For centuries, schooling was controlled across the United States by locally elected school boards who sought to have schools that reflected the community's values and needs. These were not always successful. Considering only about 5 to 10 percent of registered voters actually participate in a school board election when such elections are held independently from presidential campaigns, one can imagine how easy it is for a fringe faction of the community to take control of the schools—away from professional educators such as teachers, principals, and superintendents (assuming that the superintendent is not elected also, as is still the case in some districts). The trials and tribulations of school boards are noted throughout history. Mark Twain once said: "On the eighth day, God invented fools. But that was only for practice. Then came school boards." Yes, school boards do make mistakes, usually when they try to micromanage schools and principals; they are at their best when they do what they are designed to do—develop policy. These trials and tribulations have contributed to states gaining control of local schooling. Most school districts receive about one-half of their funding from state governments, the rest through local taxation, usually property taxes. A small percentage, loosely connected to the level of poverty in the district, comes from federal sources such as Title I.

With state control of schooling comes mandated curriculum, a movement that is a result of such publications as *A Nation at Risk* and other instances of the battering of schools from the various media. These curricula are set by noneducators who are ignorant of the needs of our students and perhaps of our workforce and society. This standardization of education, which is a result of the accountability movement, is also a result of a lack of trust of educators by noneducators. Although I am not advocating that noneducators dictate to educators what it is they should be doing to prepare students for the future, I am proposing that noneducator stakeholders at each school help shape policy. The result, of course, could be changing policies from year to year as the make-up of the different school-based policy teams changes. So what? In fact, this is good if it requires the structure of the school to become more organic, more flexible to meet the changing needs and desires of the stakeholders. It is, after all, this lack of ability to meet the needs and desires of all stakeholders that has led to the accountability movement. If schools and school systems had not been stuck in the industrial age, perhaps the public would have had no desire to pull them back to the "golden age" of education, the mythical times when most of us went to school when everything is remembered through the proverbial rose-colored glasses.

Because schools have not changed with the times, the stakeholders of the schools and school systems do indeed have reason to mandate change. Unfortunately (and this is not nearly a strong enough term), the stakeholders do not realize *why* schools are failing; they can only assume that they fail because they are not doing enough of what they have always done. Noneducators, and most educators as well, cannot comprehend what it is schools should be doing and what they should look like in order to prepare our children for the global age. As Toffler noted, very few of us can actually comprehend the wave of civilization in which we live until we have actually lived it. The mandated curricula are a result of a lack of understanding of this new wave of civilization by noneducators and educators alike. The curricula are simply a way to ensure that schools do more of what they have always done: prepare our children for the industrial age and widen the gap between the haves and the have-nots.

We do need the input of stakeholders in our schools and in our school systems. It is, however, the duty of informed educators to ensure that they have "schooled" the stakeholders as to how we must educate children for the global age. What we recall from our schools days is no longer relevant in the global age. We cannot expect our parents, business and community leaders, and the students to understand this. It is our moral obligation to establish and nurture schools and schooling for the global age, and it is our duty as educators to educate the public as well.

ROLES OF STAKEHOLDERS

In this section, the roles of each of the various stakeholders are explored, based on how the Swedes explained these roles: by first explaining the rights and the obligations of each. In chapter 7, I connect the roles of those in the schools with the needs of global-age organizations and the global village.

Schools

The rights of the school, including everyone who works or attends the school, are that they receive both the economic and moral support from the immediate community in which it resides as well as by the local, state, and federal governments. Support must be based on the unique needs of each school, which are determined by the stakeholders in the school through the facilitation of the principal. A school that has a high poverty level would need a significant amount of financial support from various levels of government, but would also need local community support in other ways, such as volunteerism. Schools with high-risk students (those identified as at risk of dropping out of school due to learning disabilities or other disadvantages such as poverty) would demand local, state, and federal funding at higher levels than those schools that have high percentages of students from higher socioeconomic families.

At this point, I think it pertinent to briefly address the issues of funding and segregation. After the 1896 *Plessy v. Ferguson* Supreme Court ruling (which said separate but equal facilities, including schools, were legal) until it was overturned by the 1954 *Brown v. Topeka Board of Education* case, black children and white children generally attended different schools. It was not until the busing era of the late 1960s and early '70s that something was finally done about segregation. These segregated schools were not equal, few would argue, but alarmingly we have allowed segregation to continue in a different form—that is, "white flight" to the suburbs. African Americans, Latinos, and other underprivileged populations are left in dilapidated, ancient structures with deficient materials and sometimes poor quality of teaching. (The teaching in urban schools often is more industrial age than in the suburbs and rural areas). States have developed formulae to ensure that all school districts get equitable funding—or at least that is the intention. Even if the formulae appear fair and just, it is likely that a high-SES suburban school will spend much more on each student than its low-SES urban counterpart. As much as I endorse diversity in communities and in schools, having a true community school is far too important to bus underprivileged youth to suburban schools. In fact, the concept of moving a child from his or her neighborhood school to a "good" school—whether it is public or private—and then expecting that child to succeed just because of the new school's record of "achievement" (usually measured by suspect test scores) is not valid.

Some individuals and organizations wish to privatize public schools, and anything else that employs government workers so that the laws of supply and demand can take over and "save" education. Vouchers, opportunity scholarships, or whatever is the current term for allowing children and parents to abandon their community schools, have been found to be insufficient to help underprivileged children. In fact, many choose to go back to their original school once they have been at the "successful" school. The answer is not to punish poor schools by luring away their children or bribing them with monetary incentives to perform better on dubious standardized tests; the answer is to improve schools with high poverty by changing everything about them. Change must come to their structure, management style, the teaching strategies, and the roles of all the stakeholders in and outside that school.

Schools have the right to be supported, but just as responsibility is tied to trust, obligation is connected to the right to be supported sufficiently. The obligation of schools is to be open and accepting of the stakeholders' needs, desires, and opinions. How can this be done when a school has 4,000 students and is being pulled in every direction by the community and the parents? First of all, a school should not have 4,000 students, but schools can, if restructured properly, meet the needs and desires of all their stakeholders through individualizing of learning. With individualization of the curricula and employment of teaching strategies that ensure individualization, parent and student complaints dwindle, and those that are left are easily resolved. As the students and parents become satisfied customers, so do the community, the media, and the politicians who "call off the dogs" (the accountability movement).

Sound simple? It is and it is not. The Swedes went through an immense nationwide education reform in 1994 to establish this type of individualization, among other global-age schooling strategies. Five years later, I began to see the results, and they were truly amazing. I know that if a small nation of 9 million people can accomplish such a feat, so can each of our fifty states. We simply have to call on our fabled "Yankee ingenuity." Of course, other obligations of the school, such as ensuring that students learn what is important to know and are able to do in the global age, are part of the restructuring that is connected to individualization of learning. As we will see later, the formation of schools within schools allows for a family-like atmosphere of caring that ensures a safe and effective learning environment.

Last, schools must guarantee that all students gradually learn to take responsibility for their learning. This is also a requirement of teachers, parents, and the students themselves. Students can only begin to be responsible if they learn in an environment that nurtures responsibility. Too often in our schools, the rules are so rigid and the supervision so tight that students do not need to take responsibility. Learning is forced upon them and into them, and the punishment for nonconformity so harsh that they either "get in line" or leave. With an environment that fosters responsibility comes the understanding of democratic principles that provides the foundation of knowledge necessary for the students to become active members of our democratic process. By learning in a democratic environment and through active engagement in this environment, students, upon leaving school, will expect and demand true democracies where they work and live. One day we may have elections where the vast majority of our eligible voters participate and do so as informed citizens concerned about the community's needs and understand that these needs are intertwined with their own. That will mark the beginning of a public democracy where the needs and desires of all are truly considered and hopefully met.

The role of the school, therefore, is to be a global-age entity—one that promotes learning by all (including its staff), utilizes Theory Y type management (which will be explained in chapter 7) so that all stakeholders have a voice in the direction the school takes and how it proceeds in this direction, and is organic in structure so that it can be responsive to the needs of the stakeholders. In contrast, the role of second-wave schools (the schools we know) is to ensure the status quo by severely controlling those within them, including teachers and administrators, so that those who are currently powerful will remain so and those who are disenfranchised will continue to be disempowered.

Students

The first right of students is the assurance that their time in school will not be wasted performing irrelevant tasks or learning irrelevant material. All that is to be learned should be useful in "navigating the seas" of the new era. All curricula developers and the teachers who choose to facilitate the learning of this content must be able to answer the proverbial student question, "What am I going to use this for?" If the question cannot be answered (beyond that it is something that will be tested or that it is part of a state-mandated knowledge standard), then either the teacher should not ask the student to learn it or it should not be in the curriculum. Granted, not all knowledge can be immediately used to serve students in their lives, but the road to that use should always be visible and readily explained.

It is also the students' right to be educated in an organization that is modeled after those in the third wave, not the second. How can a person be expected to thrive in a global organization if he or she has never experienced one?

Another right is to be trusted by adults in the schools, trusted to do what is uniquely "right" for them and their own learning.

Students also have the right to express their opinions and have those opinions addressed when appropriate; with this right comes the right to be educated so that they know how and when to express these opinions, and especially how to formulate them intelligently.

Students' obligations in global schools are the greatest of all the stakeholders' obligations because they must be the ones who shoulder most of the responsibility to learn, not the teachers or parents. The old saying "You can lead a horse to water, but you cannot make it drink" has an addendum in education: "but you can make it thirsty." Granted, one of the most important roles of teachers is that of the motivator, but even with all the strategies and even trickery employed by the teacher, one cannot learn without an emotional commitment by the learner. The responses by Swedish high school students during my first trip to Sweden still amaze me. As noted earlier, when I asked several students individually all over a particular campus in northern Sweden why they chose to stay in school and study or work on a project with other students when no one was forcing them to do so, the reply was invariably, "It is my responsibility to learn." High school is not compulsory in Sweden, and teachers rarely take attendance. In addition, students often have several hours between classes, time that they would spend studying. Through the reinforcing of values education based on democratic learning environments, Swedish students take responsibility to learn (not all, I am sure, but indeed a higher percentage than American students). I have tremendous faith in our American children. They, too, can be responsible if allowed to gradually take on responsibility of their learning as well as their behavior. Value-driven curricula can produce value-laden citizens.

Essentially, the role of the student in global-age schools is to be an active participant in his or her own learning as well as an active participant in the democratic environment created by the schools. This requires our students to become responsible not only for themselves but for others in their school and larger communities. Our system of democracy, or at least the system that we should have, depends on this acceptance of responsibility.

Teachers

Teaching is historically a low-paying career, perhaps due to it being dominated by females. The responsibilities and expectations of teachers today are much greater than in the past and will only increase with the advent of global-age schooling. Therefore, teachers have the right to be supported financially with pay that is commensurate with their levels of education and the stressful work required of them. Unions are crucial in gaining this right. First, however, unions must abandon their industrial-age labor tactics. Teachers do not carry lunch buckets and punch time clocks. (Wait a minute, many do! But they should not.) If they are to be professionals and given autonomy to make their own decisions about what they do, then they must not associate themselves with bargaining units that treat them as line workers. Unions can and must transform themselves into professional organizations that support teachers' working conditions rather than merely fight with administrators about pay. Poor working conditions are the most commonly mentioned reason for teachers leaving the field (Ingersoll 2002). Working conditions will change dramatically if administrators use quality management styles and help the stakeholders develop global-age school organizations that are worker friendly. The union's work will and should be much more that of an intellectual professional organization than a get-in-your-face negotiator. I believe union officials would greatly appreciate this change in their role.

As mentioned, teachers have the right to work in environments that are conducive to success in their work—that is, to help students and themselves continue to learn. With the proper management style employed by administrators and with teachers gaining the understanding of how to develop the proper learning organization, work environments will indeed change for the better. Retention of teachers, a problem all over but especially apparent in urban areas, should become a concern of the past. (Contrary to popular belief propagated by the various media, there are very few teacher shortages. Typically each year, twice as many new teachers graduate from various colleges of education than there are teaching vacancies in this nation. Most of these new graduates find work in other fields, but often "return" to the classroom after a downsizing or during a midlife crisis. Shortages are very much a reality in many urban settings, especially in special education and high-level math and science. These shortages are due to lack of retention; urban teachers too often "burn out" and flee to suburban schools or to other professions.)

The teacher's obligations are to ensure that all students use their experiences in order to learn to the best of their abilities. Notice I do not mention "teaching" children. That term connotes a transfer of knowledge model system that is denounced by Freire (1973; 1970) and others, especially constructivists (e.g., Applefield, Huber, and Moallem 2000; Howard, McGee, and Schwartz 2000; Marlowe and Page 1998; Shapiro 2000). Another obligation is to be active in the governance of the school, not simply allowing administrators to make decisions and then condemning them later if these decisions are unpopular. At one school where I worked, administrators solicited teacher input, received little, and were greatly criticized by teachers for their decisions. Most schools, I must admit, do not even ask for teacher input; when they do, teachers often ignore the request. If teachers are not willing to take the responsibility to engage in decision making when asked, then the school will reflect the state of our nation as a whole where only special interest groups' messages are heard.

The role of the global-age teacher is multifaceted. First, the teacher must be a facilitator of student learning, a role that requires one to be an exceptional motivator of students, assuming that the changing school structure has not instilled internal motivation into each and every student (a safe assumption, I am afraid). The teacher must be a collaborator with other professionals within and outside the school, constantly gaining understanding of his or her students as well as best teaching practices. Teacher-as-researcher might be asking too much for every teacher to accept; however, I believe it essential that teachers be able to use inquiry to expand their knowledge about learning—identifying a problem, asking the correct questions, finding solutions and answers, acting upon these solutions and answers, and most important, reflecting. The teacher as a mere "fount of knowledge" is an antiquated ideal, one that should have disappeared along with the industrial age.

The global-age teacher is much more than his or her industrial-age counterpart; in fact, the term "teacher" is not appropriate for this new professional. I hesitate to use "facilitator" to describe teachers because of the connotations that are somehow linked to it by teachers, connotations that may infer a less knowledgeable or powerful person than the "teacher." Perhaps the use of "learning promoter" rather than teacher would be more acceptable. Learning promoter has at least two benefits: (1) it better describes the roles of the teacher in the global school because he or she does indeed promote student learning as well as his or her own learning and (2) "teacher," despite the efforts by teachers' unions and other teacher advocacy groups in the past decade or so, is still not a well-respected term or position in the eyes of the public.

Too many believe teaching to be an easy job where so-called professionals are merely babysitters who must stay just a page ahead of the students in the textbooks and who work short hours and get summers off with long vacations during the year. Well, I must admit, that does describe many teachers in the industrial age. We all may have had several teachers like this in our school days, and those of us in education have worked with a few like this. "Learning promoter" is at once more positive than "teacher" with all its baggage, connotes motivation, and gives no indication that the person is merely someone who transfers knowledge from one place (his or her head or a textbook) into the student's head. (I toyed with "learning manager" but "manager" has industrial-age connotations and is very bureaucratic in function.)

Principals

Although most schools have other administrators on site besides the principal, I refer to all site-based administrators as simply the "principal." Principals have the right to be supported by the district offices as leaders of nearly autonomous organizations. While it is important that the district has a vision and certain guiding policies written by the school board, principals must be granted a large degree of freedom so that they can meet the unique needs of their schools' communities both inside the schools and surrounding the schools. The principal also has the right to have final power to hire or remove an incompetent employee or one who simply does not fit the needs of the organization or the students.

Principals are obligated to follow the vision of the school district as well as they can while still helping guide their schools toward meeting the needs of their local stakeholders. This, of course, calls for a new style of manager, one who is willing to be flexible and ensure power is given, as much as possible, to the stakeholders. Like the teacher, principals are obligated to promote learning in students, but principals must also promote learning within the entire organization. And the principal's office is where "the buck stops." I contend that schools have one person who accepts full responsibility although conversely is not entirely responsible for the actions of those in the school. In other words, each person, group, or team of persons within the school organization should be responsible for his/her/their actions; yet one individual must be strong enough to assume responsibility for the organization as a whole. Therefore, principals are ultimately responsible for the functioning of the entire school without minimalizing the actions of those with whom they work. This new role demands a different type of leadership than is found in a second-wave organization, a leadership that will be discussed in some detail in the next chapter.

As with the term *teacher*, *principal* has negative connotations with the public. Principals are too often deemed to be (1) the persons to whose offices misbehaving students are sent when teachers have lost their patience, (2) expendable middle-level managers who are to simply enforce district policy while keeping all stakeholders at bay so the district offices do not have to be bothered, and (3) those who ensure that no negative publicity comes from their school (see no evil, hear no evil, speak no evil).

Therefore, I propose the use of "organization support leader" (OSL). This new job title calls attention to the primary functions of global-age principals: support and lead. Principals must support teachers, noninstructional personnel, and students to ensure that learning is taking place throughout the organization. They are specialists in organization support, more so than any other person in the building; otherwise, they would not be in that position—at least in theory. The days of promoting teachers into administrative roles based on the "good old boy" system, where connections among former coaches ensure one's promotion, are hopefully gone. The job is far too important in the global-age school to be given to someone as a political favor or a reward for building a winning football program. The OSL's role as leader is that of facilitator of learning for the entire building. The organizational support leader also functions as a visionary leader, one who ensures that everyone in the organization shares the vision of the school organization.

School Districts

The 14,000-plus public school districts in the United States are generally supported by local property taxes and by state support, as noted previously; usually, very little support comes from the federal government (typically less than 10 percent). The right of school districts is to be supported by the local community (those who pay taxes) by ensuring that they receive what is needed to create and sustain schools that are conducive to student learning for the global age. Tax referendums, within reason, need to be backed by community leaders, including those who do not have children in the public schools. (This latter group reaps the benefits of living in an educated society. It is appalling that some senior citizens whose children are now grown and some people without children believe that they should not have to support the schools as they do not directly use these services. This is both ignorant and selfish. Our entire society is affected by the quality of our schools, either positively or negatively.)

School districts also have the right to adequate funding from the state level to help support their unique needs. Districts are too often forced to follow state-designed curricula and standards, and to implement a testing system without the appropriate funds to support these mandates. I am vehemently opposed to state-imposed, lock-step curricular mandates and their accompanying high-stakes testing because these greatly inhibit each school's ability to meet the learning needs of its students. A few years ago, a Swedish friend summarized my school and school district as "having all the obligations without any control." State governments are feeling the same way with the ESEA mandates; they are forced to implement a system of accountability that they did not ask to have. Of course, if schooling were operated in a global-age manner, schools would not need to worry themselves with intrusive state and federal mandates.

At this point, it is important to answer the question, "Is global-age schooling more expensive than industrial-age schooling?" It is and it is not. It is more expensive, at least initially, in that services must be steered toward those who are most in need. Students at risk often require smaller classes and, as I point out in chapter 7, smaller schools. Smaller classes and smaller schools may indeed be more labor intensive than the existing enormous campuses of three, four, even five thousand students with their overcrowded classes of forty-plus students, all too common in urban and suburban districts. These costs, however, could be balanced by the lack of need of excessive supervision. As students become more responsible and better motivated because of schools becoming relevant to their lives and the world around them, the need for supervision decreases. Older students can come and go from the school without the need for security guards at every entrance. The need for adults in the form of teachers, administrators, security guards, or actual police will be drastically reduced with the responsibility and trust found in a democratic learning environment. A class of thirty may seem like fifteen to a teacher when he or she does not have to supervise all thirty at once, trusting many to work independently elsewhere. Sound too good to be true? Before my visits to Sweden, I would have said "Yes." Now I know that it can be done.

School districts also have the right to be supported from below, that is, from the schools/ Schools should be primarily concerned with their own local learning community, seeking to meet the needs of their students and other stakeholders. But schools also have a larger community in which they reside: the district. Having worked in a district of 175,000 students, I can understand an individual school's unwillingness to support a huge bureaucracy that is often faceless and seemingly unsupportive of the individual school. To implement the global-age schooling model, it would be necessary for larger districts (over 15,000 students) to be divided into smaller autonomous districts, where each would have an autonomous regional superintendent to support each of his or her schools without the fear of being micromanaged by the central superintendent. The central district, conversely, can expect all regional districts and the schools within them to support their vision of schooling and learning. No school should stray too far from the guiding vision, especially if it is one that supports global schooling.

This guiding vision is the main obligation of the superintendent who must facilitate the development and the marketing of the vision. Superintendents are obligated to the policies developed by the school board, yet a strong superintendent will ensure that these policies follow the overall vision shared by the community and the schools in that community. A grave mistake for any school district, especially a large one, is to dictate a vision that is not held by the school communities. Peter Senge (1990) warns that visions that are not embraced by all in an organization, but are forced upon them, will be undermined at the lowest levels. I once worked for a school district that had an outstanding, progressive vision for schooling, yet the vision was mandated by those at the highest levels of administration. As good as the vision was, the teachers did not feel they owned that vision and began to resent it—even the ones who believed it was in the best interest of their students.

Parents

Those of us who have children in schools have the right to be welcome in those schools and to be kept abreast of what is happening schoolwide as well as with our own children. The elimination of the antiquated grading system will help in this communication. Schools as well as children are traditionally graded A through F in our public school systems. What does an A tell us? It depends on who is giving the grade. I firmly believe that all is relative where grading is concerned, despite the proliferation of rubrics in the education community over the past few decades, an attempt to objectify what will always be subjective. Grade inflation is a concern of traditionalists, but does it really matter what grade a student receives? More important than an arbitrary grade is what the student has learned. This can only be done using authentic assessments, that is, those that actually reflect what the student knows and can do compared to pencil-and-paper tests that simply show what the student could remember that certain day. Descriptions of what the child is like in school and what the child is learning are more valuable than our ineffective traditional grading systems.

In Sweden, grades are not given until noncompulsory upper secondary school. Parents are kept abreast of their child's progress through parent–teacher conferences. It must be noted that the level of trust is so high in that country that teachers I spoke with could not recall an angry parent telephoning them or coming to the school looking for an argument. Perhaps this trust is because of effective school-home communication. As a former assistant principal, a good portion of my time and energy was spent mediating between angry parents and teachers. With the possible exception of extracurricular activities, school personnel did not see parents unless something was deemed wrong. We have a long way to go to build this level of trust between parents and schools. I do not believe parents are to blame for this lack of trust; it is the irrelevant school systems that are the culprits. If we as educators were actually fulfilling our moral obligation of preparing students for the global age, parents would have very few reasons not to trust us.

The obligations of the parents are simply to be good parents. Perhaps the use of "simply" is misleading, but parents' obligations have really not changed much in the global age. They are to provide their children with basic food and shelter and, most important, love. Emotional security might be more important now than it was a few generations ago because of the rapid changes in our society. Adults are usually understandably ignorant of the expectations of the global age and the direction it is taking us. They themselves need emotional security, but our children need this security even more. When speaking with teachers who have taught for more than thirty years, they say the real difference between the students today as compared to when they began their careers is that students now need much more attention. An emphasis on meeting children's emotional security needs may help alleviate this lack of attention. As classrooms and schools become larger and larger, teachers and other school personnel cannot give students as much individual attention as they need. The parents must make up for this. Of course, if we establish schools that resemble caring learning communities, schools can begin to help parents meet the emotional security needs of students.

Parents are also obligated to support change in the schools. The schools they attended were designed to prepare them for the industrial age—a preparation that was most likely useless for them, resulting in much of the distrust for our schools. Although parents might or might not understand the needs of the global economy, they must trust schools that are changing into global-age organizations. I can understand how it would be comforting in this time of great societal turmoil to see that our schools resemble the ones we attended. We can count on that comfort every time we enter a public school. The only difference between the schools we attended and today's schools might be new technology (and even that is probably out of date). The basic structure and teaching methods are the same as they have been for a century. Unfortunately, these schools that resemble the ones we attended are irrelevant to the global age. Parents must forgo the need for the nostalgic comfort of industrial-age schools and embrace real school change, as well as trust schools to implement change, and participate in and positively support the school in this change.

Local Communities

The community adjacent to and directly affected by each school also has rights. These rights may be the most important in that schooling is an institution in our society that has taken on more and more importance in the past few generations. I hesitate to use the phrase "breakdown of the family" because the changes in family patterns I believe are due primarily to outside societal influences, specifically economic changes. The family has not necessarily broken down as much as it has changed in form and possibly in function. Single-parent households can cause great emotional and economic stress to children but so can both parents needing to work in order to maintain the standard of living that was reached by a one-wage-earner household during the height of the industrial age. Mass media advertising has convinced us that we must possess bigger houses, more complex cars, and the latest technology. If we were to live the same lifestyle in regards to possessions as did our grandparents, many of our households would not need to have two wage earners. But let us consider the underprivileged in our society. They may be worse off than ever before in recent history. They need as many as possible working in the household due to falling wages (adjusted to inflation) in addition to their exclusion from participating in the global economy. Indeed, changes in society have altered the American family unit over the past two or three generations.

This alteration of the family in both structure and function has also changed the focus of schooling as an institution. "Full-service schools"—schools that offer services to low-SES clientele such as medical care and other social services—have increased in number for two decades. But these are still not common enough. The typical low-SES school must somehow accept the responsibility of filling in where the family cannot: free and reduced-price breakfasts and lunches, before- and after-school child care, and the teaching of societal values. I believe this last is essential for all global-age schools, but the first two must continue until the business community and politicians are willing to narrow the chasm between the haves and have-nots.

The right of the local community is to have schools that enable students to learn basic and advanced academics to the best of their abilities while promoting societal and global values. These values are, of course, to include democracy, trust, and responsibility. Communities should also expect that their schools are safe havens from drugs and violence, societal plagues that are found in all parts of our nation—rural, suburban, and urban. The fostering of and focus on values education should help alleviate these plagues found inside and outside schools, ending the need for schools to resemble prisons where all who enter are justifiably scrutinized and, worse yet, students are contained in them against their wills.

The obligations of the community are intertwined with the community's role and include support of the schools both financially and spiritually. Tax referendums that are needed to enhance student learning (versus those that simply propagate bureaucracies) should first be examined by the community and then voted on appropriately. Involvement in schools should be a civic duty akin to voting in elections, although I realize the latter is not deemed too important in our private democracy. Stakeholders from the community should be welcome in the schools, and schools should allow for formal and casual opportunities to visit them. I ate in a school cafeteria in Sweden where the public was welcome. They simply came in as they would any cafeteria-style restaurant and ate with the teenage students. No school personnel, other than the food servers, were present. This scenario reflects two possible outcomes of global-age schooling: openness and trust.

GOALS OF GLOBAL-AGE SCHOOLS

Schools' goals, simply put, are to prepare children for the global age, a time when change is constant, rapid, and unpredictable. All school stakeholders should strive toward establishing an environment where all students can learn to the best of their abilities. This all sounds very honorable and probably familiar, yet with our current system—the one that has been in place for at least a century—this is impossible. We teach to the masses. This is one of the primary malfunctions in our education system.

First, "we teach" implies that this is something we do to the children. Learning scholars understand that students cannot learn at a high level any content that is transferred from a person or textbook into the learner without the student accepting this knowledge as legitimate. If students are not convinced that what they are to learn is worth knowing, can positively affect their lives (or the lack of knowing can have a negative effect), then the students will not learn the material at a high level. The learners can, as evidenced by scare tactics used by drill sergeants and teachers who are "wanna-be" drill sergeants, memorize and regurgitate low-level understanding of material. This is the crux of standardized testing for both students and teachers. But of what good is that learning? None, except to pass a test that most likely does not measure actual learning. The ancient Greek saying "No learning takes place without an emotional commitment from the learner" does not include, as I have pointed out to many teachers over the years, the emotions connected to fear and hate.

A proper learning environment is one where fear is driven out, as W. Edwards Deming advocated. The learner must feel safe not just to walk the hallways without being physically or verbally attacked but also to make mistakes as he or she learns. When observing teachers, one of the environmental items I first seek is whether or not the students comfortably contribute their opinions in the class. This, I do believe, is a sign of a true democracy. Most teachers, however, do not allow for such opinions. The only remarks they want from the students are the parroting of "correct" answers from the textbooks or of the teacher's own "vast wisdom." This parroting of answers reflects the banking system of education that Freire warned about. It establishes no real or usable learning, as when a student merely pulls knowledge that is temporarily "banked" in his or her brain and deposits it onto a test or verbally to the teacher. (A psychologist I once knew argued with me that no knowledge is actually ever lost, it is merely difficult to access. Even if we were to find a way to access all knowledge presented to us, of what use is low-level knowledge?)

A proper learning environment for the global age, which is and will be dominated by democracies and dependent upon their proliferation and continuance, is one where students do not fear to state their own opinions, opinions formulated and molded not from one established authority (the curriculum) but from a myriad of sources and sifted about by the learner based on his or her own experiences. (This follows constructivist theory and I argue in the next chapter that it must be the learning philosophy of the global school.) How else can we ensure that all will learn when we are confronted with more and more diverse student populations? Teaching to the masses assumes that all students have the same experiences and learning capabilities at the same age. This is a factory-style industrial-age mentality in which we are so ensconced that we cannot even comprehend another way of schooling, I am afraid.

Establishing this type of learning environment might enhance our students' abilities to become tolerant toward others and their opinions and cultures. If all students' viewpoints are held as valid, or at least respected, intolerance toward others will be expelled from our schools. I might be taking a Pollyanna-like stance, but if we can establish such values in the schools, would not this carry over into the world outside of schools?

Most of us understand that what our students bring into the schools from their lives has the greatest effect on their learning. It would be irresponsible to ignore that many of our students do not have the privileges of some others, privileges that will help them to learn at a higher level. Anthropologists refer to these privileges as "cultural capital." Many of our students are victims of poverty, a condition that our society as a whole does not care to tackle, as we merely place bandages on it with a poorly planned and funded welfare system. Instead of confronting the real roots of poverty, we bandage the people just enough to keep them from robbing us blind and then go on to blame the schools for not educating them and therefore keeping them in such a condition. Of course, schools as industrial-age relics cannot be anything more than the proverbial mirrors of society. The global school can be much more: it can be a catalyst for change that can lead to helping other aspects of our society to, among other necessary endeavors, eradicate poverty. If the first goal of schooling is to establish effective learning environments, then the second goal is to act as a catalyst of change in society, change that will produce and sustain a public democracy.

By fostering values in our students, values that will help our fellow beings instead of simply helping ourselves, we can create changes that can ensure that we continue to evolve as a society. I was ashamed of myself as an educator and of what my nation had allowed its schools to become when I saw in Sweden that the people, especially teenagers, were much more aware of the world around them and the conditions that exist. I felt compelled to explain to the Swedes that we as a people hold a myopic view of ourselves and our world. We do not comprehend what our fallacies are and what effects these have on the rest of the world. Our military and economic strengths cause us to be watched closely by others in both the developed and the developing world. The developing countries often try to establish a system of government and economics based on ours, which is quite flattering for us. The developed nations, however, do not hold us up as models to emulate because they are cognizant of our many shortcomings, most of which might be caused by our inexperienced society—inexperienced when compared to European and Asian cultures.

In Sweden, I felt as if I were "dragging my knuckles" when told of the superior social services they offered their citizens, social services that included a far superior system of schooling. I have stated before that I am an American and am proud of my nation and for what it stands, or at least for what it was meant to stand. I do indeed love the people of our nation as well as all those in the global village. Because of this pride and love, I feel compelled to write this book and to work toward establishing schools that truly make a difference in our nation. It is very difficult for Americans to swallow our pride long enough to admit that we have made mistakes and need to enact the necessary changes. Liberals often correctly cite these mistakes but are too busy criticizing to offer useful help or criticize so sharply that their viewpoints are not taken as valid. (I should know because I was once a conservative who often winced at liberal criticism.) Conservatives, on the other hand, want to neither see nor hear any criticism because the way our society is today has served them quite well—or at least so they believe.

In essence, the goals of establishing effective learning environments for pragmatic and deep learning as well as the establishment of schools as catalysts of change in our society are truly our moral obligation to our children, to us adults, and to the world. We cannot continue to settle for an irrelevant system of schooling, one that perpetuates inequity and antiquated skills. Schools can no longer accept their current status as mirrors of society; they must establish themselves as one of the most powerful engines of change in our society, engines that can ensure the fostering of citizens who can and will intelligently participate in a true democracy.

SEVEN

Vision for Global-Age Schooling

A sweeping educational reform in 1994 resulted in two national curricula that are essentially a vision of schooling experiences for Swedish children living in a globalized society within and beyond the Swedish political borders and culture. Municipalities, principals, teachers, and especially students are trusted to implement this vision based on their needs and desires. Accountability rests at the local level; the school system is part of the local government, not a separate entity as is typical in the United States. Therefore, all local government officials hold responsibility. (At a school board meeting I attended, a local representative from each of Sweden's seven major political parties shared with the public his or her party's perspectives on the local schools and the direction in which they were to go.) The only stringent national accountability measure consists of an exit exam at the end of compulsory education. Trust of local political and educational institutions is vital to the national education system.

In chapter 6, I laid out a model for U.S. schooling in the global age. This chapter describes in more detail some of the qualities of the global-age schooling model addressed in the previous chapter, all the while endeavoring to express a relevant vision for schooling in today's society and for schooling in our future.

AN EDUCATIONAL PHILOSOPHY
TO EMBRACE

The study I conducted in central Sweden was for my dissertation; upon my return to the United States, I began to quickly write the required chapter that was to report my findings. When my supervising professor read the rough draft, he concluded that I had witnessed three "constructivist" schools. I felt embarrassed, as I was not very familiar with the term *constructivist*, having only heard it used in passing during my graduate studies. Not wanting to seem foolish, I resisted the temptation of engaging him in further conversation, and ran off to the campus library to find as much information as I could on the subject, including my professor's newly published book about constructivist leadership in schools. After perusing a few volumes, I found that constructivism was a philosophy that I had been living as an educator; moreover, I wondered if the constructivist philosophy of education was the basis of Swedish education reforms. No reference was made to constructivism, however, in my search of the literature on Swedish school reform, yet they had embraced constructivism, including the teaching strategies and learning environments that are conducive to this philosophy. This philosophy, I contend, is one of the keys to restructuring U.S. schools to produce the global citizen-worker.

Constructivism has been one of the most written about and perhaps the most revered learning theory for the past decade. The ideas and values it holds were well known to me even though the term was not. In short, constructivism is the belief that one learns content through his or her own lens of experience. If, for example, Johnny and Joan are students in a class sitting side by side, and they both are presented the same information from the teacher regarding Steinbeck's *The Grapes of Wrath*, they would understand it differently. Johnny's background, being a bit different from Joan's, would cause him to filter the symbolism of the Jobes family heading West through his own unique experiences. Joan would do the same, but because her experiences as a female and, perhaps, from another race, religion, culture, or socioeconomic background are different from Johnny's, her understanding of this symbolism would most likely differ from his. Therefore, constructivists argue, a teacher cannot expect all thirty-five students in her English classroom to gain the identical understanding of Steinbeck's symbolism from a reading of *The Grapes of Wrath* unless, of course, the teacher is simply "spoon-feeding" answers to the students. But that is not meaningful learning because it is not "owned" by the learner, because she did not come to the conclusions by herself. She is taking the teacher's learning or, more likely, the textbook's learning, as gospel. Memorization also does not allow students to reflect upon the information; Joan would have no emotional commitment to this knowledge because she would have no ownership of it. Constructivism allows for the learner to take ownership by learning through his or her own life experiences, thus allowing for a deeper emotional commitment.

Constructivism is nothing new, despite traditionalists' claim that it is the latest education fad that will soon die out, as all education fads seem to do. Its roots can be traced as far back as Socrates but most scholars would agree that the most influential works contributing to the genesis of constructivism are of the Swiss psychologist Jean Piaget and the American philosopher and educator John Dewey. Piaget advocated a moral reasoning view of learning, a reasoning that took place through students' interpersonal relationships (i.e., socializing). It must be noted that most educators think of Piaget in terms of his famous stages of learning, stages that also play an important part of constructivism. Dewey, perhaps the most important figure in education in the last century, advocated active, pragmatic learning. Students learn best when they actually do something rather than sitting passively and absorbing information from a teacher. This learning must also be relevant to the students' lives; otherwise, it will not be deemed pragmatic. Making learning relevant involves allowing students to understand through the lens of their lifetime of experiences. This, constructivists contend, is the only way of truly "knowing." Most learning takes place through interpersonal communication, much to the chagrin of textbook publishers, and this communication is a large part of one's life experiences.

Although technically an epistemology, I contend that constructivism is actually a philosophy of education, one in which teaching strategies and learning environments have been identified as being conducive to its goals. I refer to constructivist teaching strategies as those that are active, require dialogue, allow student autonomy in choice and control, and are flexible. Constructivist environments are student centered in that the teacher is not the focus—physically, emotionally, or intellectually—in the classroom. This type of school environment probably would not look like those to which the reader is accustomed, just as most work environments today do not resemble those of the industrial age. Straight rows of desks facing the teacher at a chalkboard or overhead would most likely not be seen in a constructivist classroom. The teacher would blend in with the students and take on the role of colearner instead of the omniscient one who spouts a fountain of knowledge for the students to soak in. In fact, a teacher's desk is merely a workstation that need not be even present in the room. A constructivist teacher is too busy working with students at their locations rather than sitting at a desk. The concept of place takes on a whole new meaning in that students are not confined to a desk or even a classroom.

I noted earlier that some Swedish high schools had built glassed-in student conference rooms so that students could leave the confinement of their cells (classrooms) and work without interruptions. (This is now being proposed in the small schools movement supported by the ESEA and the Gates Foundation.) Of course, I am reminded by teachers and administrators, we cannot do this in the United States because our students cannot be trusted to work without supervision. No, they probably cannot because they are the products of industrial-age classroom environments. Given the threat of lawsuits due to the misuse of the in loco parentis statutes where the educator is given all the responsibility of the parent at the school, we could not leave them to find out. I did, of course, witness hundreds of Swedish high school students eat peacefully without adult supervision. As an American, I am appalled and embarrassed that our children and adolescents are not able, or at least not given the opportunity, to act in a civilized manner in an unsupervised setting. The reason may be the vicious cycle in which we find ourselves: the more we supervise, the more we need to supervise. Our students are not heathens as compared to the Swedes; they simply have not been allowed the freedom nor have they had responsibility nurtured in them. In this respect, we are neither the "land of the free" (we do not value freedom in our schools) nor are we the "home of the brave" (we do not have the courage to allow for and nurture freedom). It is ironic that our children are condemned to a state of maximum security for twelve or thirteen years only to be let loose into what may be the most liberal society in the world (at least in regards to civil liberties).

In order for teachers to accept and model constructivist practices in the classroom (and outside the classroom), they must take on different roles, as explained in chapter 6. Although constructivism requires the teacher to act as facilitator, I am a bit reluctant to use the term because

of its negative connotation among traditional educators. While conducting a grade-level meeting at a middle school once, I slipped and referred to the veteran staff of sixth-grade teachers as the "f-word" (facilitators). One gentleman stood up in the back of the room and said that
he resented being called that as he was proud to be a teacher. I did not
accuse him or anyone else in the room of not teaching, it is just that
the term *teacher* has the connotation of being the great dispenser of
knowledge. The teacher is seen by society as one who controls students
and disperses content while the students obey and absorb, both passive
acts. Why not take the tired, much maligned term *teacher* and change
it to something like *facilitator*? Or, as I proffer in the last chapter,
knowledge promoter. As teachers have attempted to gain respect in society, they still hold on to the traditional emblems of their profession,
such as the red apple and the little red schoolhouse. This clinging to the
past is symbolic of teachers' reluctance to give control to students. A
new way of thinking about learning and *facilitating* learning is needed
if we are to change schooling so that it fosters citizens for the global age.
I believe constructivism is central to that new paradigm.

AUTONOMY OF STUDENTS AND TEACHERS

Students and teachers in Sweden are greatly involved in the interpreta-
tions of the vision handed down through the Swedish National Curricula. Each and every student from preschool through adult education
must develop an individual learning plan based on his or her interests
and perceived needs. This autonomy can lead to responsibility and increased motivation, if nurtured correctly. I am reminded by U.S. educators that we cannot simply give our students the autonomy to make their
own decisions. They are half right. Our students have been acculturated
to follow directions, often mindlessly, not questioning authority. This reflects the value of control in an industrial-age organization and management system. No, we cannot give our students the power to make their
own decisions because they do not know how to do so effectively, which
is no fault of theirs. Our system of schooling is to blame. (I refute the
concept that our children—and all people—are inherently evil and,

therefore, incapable of making moral decisions without strict controls of mind and actions.)

Our children must be given opportunities to make choices in their learning; the only choice they have today in schools is between doing what authority dictates or being punished. When our students leave K–12 education, they will be asked to make some very important choices: where to live, how to make a living, who to choose as a life partner, when to have children, and for which candidates they should vote. One of the messages coming from *A Nation at Risk* was that our young adults wander aimlessly from low-wage job to low-wage job after high school. This publication suggested that we should provide more job training in the schools. Some critics may argue that it is not the schools' concern to train people for jobs, but that it is industry's responsibility. Other critics tend to espouse the backward back-to-basics movement that is helping to render our schools irrelevant.

I contend that schools can do both: they can teach the basic skills while still fostering workforce qualities in students, and facilitate the deep understanding of content that has been missing in our children's education. We cannot do these in the current culture of distrust that does not allow students to have the power of choice. It is essential that we build and sustain democratic learning environments in our schools.

An organization best suited for the global age is one that is flexible within its environment—an environment that includes volatile markets, political upheavals, and the ever-changing needs and desires of its clients. This organization is much flatter in structure than the industrial-age bureaucracies that now dominate school systems. By "flatter," I refer to it possessing fewer layers of bureaucracy. A global-age school system would be one that is small enough that clients (parents, community members, and students) can have their message heard by those who have the power to make changes. As this might be impossible for large urban school districts where a dozen layers of bureaucracy might exist between the client and the superintendent and school board, then the answer might be to give much of the power to make important decisions to those "in the trenches," the teachers and students.

Teachers are told what and when to teach based on state, district, and federal (such as the ESEA) mandates and curricula. Rigid school schedules dictate precisely when, and where, they are to teach. Bells ring to tell them when to start and when to finish teaching, reminding one of Pavlov's dogs or, in keeping with the theme of the industrial age, of factory whistles. Administrators demand that teachers force students to learn from "bell to bell," allowing for no down time in the classroom because idle hands are the tools of you-know-who. The bell system is forced upon teachers due to tight transportation schedules and union contracts of teachers and, of course, tradition. Due to this dependency on the bell system, administrators do not have much room in class schedules for such essential items as extra planning time for teachers and crucial meetings of parents, teachers, and administrators.

But there is even more to the bell system of scheduling than these constraints: it is the unconscious adherence to the industrial-age factory model of organizations—the Frederick Taylor model circa 1900. Classes begin at ridiculously precise times such as 8:47 and end at 9:41. Besides Amtrak, who else lives by such a schedule? In the film *Election*, Matthew Broderick plays a high school social studies teacher who asks Reese Witherspoon's character to meet him at his car after school. In true factory-style education form, he instructs her to meet him at 3:20. In the "real world," he would have said "a quarter after 3:00 or 3:30." It is a wonder that he did not ask her to meet him at 3:22. Obviously, the writers of *Election* had some education advisers in order to not miss such an important nuance of today's public schools. The concept of time truly dictates our actions in industrial-age schools.

In the past, teachers often relied on textbooks to write their lesson plans. Today, they must focus their teaching on state curriculum standards that are, in turn, dictated by various national subject areas organizations. These standards are usually not correlated with the statewide tests that nearly every state administers and that the No Child Left Behind law mandates, although states are attempting to rectify this problem. Regardless, teachers are left with fewer and fewer curriculum decisions. It was bad enough when teachers relied so heavily on district- and state-approved textbooks, but now they must teach to the state standards as well as ensure that their students are able to pass the various tests that are to be administered in every grade, with the exception of eleventh and twelfth—which should be coming soon.

Yes, teachers are teaching to the test and can you blame them? Florida, for example, gives schools $100 per pupil if the school receives an A rating based on the Florida Comprehensive Assessment Test for math, reading, and writing. That amounts to $300,000 for a high school with an enrollment of 3,000 students. Is this accountability or bribery? Of course, when schools fail according to this system, Florida's governor can point to the need for privatization. If test scores increase, he can tell the public how his new education plan increases learning (when, in reality, the students were "taught to the test"). It is truly a win-win system for politicians and a lose-lose system for our students who, even if they score well on the standardized tests, probably are not obtaining relevant skills and knowledge.

How teachers teach is usually based not on current research but on peer and administrative pressure. In my first full year of teaching, I was in a high school where four rooms were connected at a common point. No doors separated the four English classes. Peer pressure made me use teaching strategies that ensured the students remained quiet so as not to disturb the other three English classes whose teachers were very traditional in their practices and whose classes were, therefore, very quiet. As a young teacher, I did not want to cause trouble so I simply conformed to the norm, despite what I knew from research to be in the best interests of my students (e.g., cooperative learning, project-based learning) that often required a relatively noisy classroom. I must add, at the beginning of that year, I was advised by a veteran English teacher to "forget all that crap they teach you in college. It doesn't work here. Just tell 'em to sit down, shut up, and listen. You're in charge!" It was not until two years later, teaching in a middle school (middle schools are much more apt to be progressive than high schools) that I had the courage to conduct my classroom as I believed it should be conducted and did not worry about what my colleagues thought.

Administrators come to teachers' classes looking mostly for control of students. It is, after all, the administrators' burden to discipline students who do not conform to the traditional teacher's demands. (At one school where I was an assistant principal working primarily with discipline, I would receive up to seventy office referrals a day, and routinely received forty each day! It got to the point that the suspension list was nearly as long as the honor roll.) Administrators have a vested interest in the teachers being able to control students. Just as teachers rarely speak about other teachers' abilities to actually promote learning in their classrooms, administrators rarely praise teachers for helping students learn. Unless, of course, it is to congratulate a teacher for helping her students increase their standardized test scores (which, I contend, does not correlate to increased learning—at least, not learning that will help the students in the global age).

Teachers do not have the autonomy to teach what they want, when they want, or even how they want due to outside mandates and influences. Most definitions of professionalism include autonomy, not lack of it. As an undergraduate, a professor upset those of us in class who were studying to be teachers when he stated that teachers were not professionals because they were not allowed autonomy. This was in the 1980s; the situation for teachers has drastically worsened since then. But we cannot simply dwell on the plight of the teachers in our control-oriented school organizations; it is the students who are controlled even more than teachers and are then expected to make those important life decisions without ever having decision-making skills nurtured or given the opportunity to make real decisions about life. Our system of schooling is a great injustice to our children, a moral injustice.

MOVING CAREFULLY TOWARD RESPONSIBILITY

U.S. schools cannot simply begin allowing students to make all their decisions. They can, however, start slowly by giving students "controlled choice" (I apologize for the oxymoron). As a middle school teacher, I began to write into my plans (and onto the chalkboard) three or four options for students to do each day. The last option was always the students' choice. If a student could convince me that his or her choice was meeting the needs of the curriculum (yes, I was forced to follow one also, just not to the degree that teachers today must), then I would allow that student to proceed with that assignment. From memory, most students stuck with one of my choices, but the choices that were developed by the students were almost always very creative and much more difficult than the activities I developed. This choice system eliminated complaints from students that they did not like what they were doing because they always had the option of devising their own learning. I hoped that my students would pass on to other teachers what I was doing and they would incorporate this strategy. It is unlikely this happened, as most teachers are afraid to give up any control due to fear of students getting the "upper hand" or of receiving administration's wrath.

One year, I used a strategy I learned in a graduate course, a strategy that allowed for students to increase their power in my classroom beginning on the first day of school in August all the way through June, while still allowing for meaningful learning to take place. On the first day, instead of growling my classroom rules at my seventh graders, I had them move into groups and brainstorm what they would like to learn that year in language arts. This included what they wanted to read, what they wanted to see on video, and what they wanted to write about. Then I asked them to develop rules and consequences for the class. I will admit that it did not work very well, despite my good intentions. By seventh grade, my students had been acculturated into a system where their opinions and decisions did not matter, acculturated to the point where they were seemingly incapable of making decisions on their own. Anecdotally, I would say that perhaps no more than 25 percent of my students actually enjoyed making their own decisions. If this were to persist into adulthood, then 75 percent of my 160 students that year would go on to become "sheep" in society, easy prey for advertisers and politicians. I spent the rest of that year nurturing decision-making skills in my students, to varying success. Sadly, as a university professor, I have found that many college students still want you to tell them exactly what to learn and what to do, even at the graduate level. These are usually very bright and capable people but, having been groomed for obedience and passivity in the American education system, they are often unwilling to take responsibility for their own learning. They, instead, want the professor to take this responsibility. After all, universities as well as K–12 schools are being held responsible for learning in the accountability movement; a movement founded on the outdated and harmful belief that knowledge is simply transferred from the teacher's head into that of the student—the "banking model" of learning as described and detested by Paulo Freire.

Years after my "democracy experiments" with my seventh-grade students, I witnessed in Sweden the types of student-empowerment activities I had attempted to employ in my classroom. Students, according to the national curriculum for compulsory schools, are encouraged to make decisions about their learning as well as their classroom environment. Teachers become true facilitators of both learning and managing the class, fostering autonomy in the students so that they can leave the schools as citizens capable of participating fully in a democracy without falling prey to the "wolves" of advertising and in various levels of our government.

CHANGING ROLES WITHIN THE SCHOOLS

Only once in the five weeks I spent in Swedish schools did I witness a teacher give a directive to a student. Thankfully, I later found this teacher to be only a substitute and . . . an American! It made me wonder if being American explained why she contrasted greatly with the other teachers, as she told the students what they should be doing, how to do it, and then scolded students for incorrect answers. Apparently, she had not taken note of how the other teachers in the building acted in their role as teachers. Or perhaps ethnocentricity kept her from desiring to change. In the late 1980s and on into the 1994 Swedish Education Act, teachers were encouraged, if not forced, by the national curricula's vision and by their own developed curricula and learning environments to become facilitators of learning. As no bells rang and no teachers stood in front of class giving directives, it was often difficult for me to ascertain when classes began and ended in Sweden. I was certain, however, that learning never stopped. Students and teachers were actively engaged nearly every moment they were in a classroom. This is the type of environment that I tried to foster in my own classrooms as a teacher in K–12 schools and again as a university professor. I was and am still somewhat unsuccessful because of the great obstacles created by our system of education. As an American, I am frightened by the bleak outlook for our democracy: apathetic citizens not wanting to participate in the democratic process; when they do, they fall prey to the mass-marketed messages of politicians, messages that have little, if any, substance. We educators can help to change this austere scenario by changing how we "do business" in schools. Perhaps the most important change we can make is in the roles we play in the schools.

The role of teachers as "dispensers of knowledge" is not only outdated but is dangerous. It promotes shallow learning and passive citizenry. Facilitating learning, despite the reluctance of teachers to accept
this role or the term *facilitate*, is precisely what teachers must do if they
are to promote a deeper understanding of content and an active citizen
of a public democracy. A facilitator of learning would structure a classroom that would not have the teacher as the center of attention. The
teacher's desk might not even be in the room, let alone facing rows of
students as a drill sergeant faces his or her troops. Walking into a classroom, one can predict with amazing accuracy what role the teacher
plays and what type of strategies the teacher employs by the way the
room is ordered. Student desks in a circle or in groups are always a good
sign. Better yet is the absence of desks at all, only tables that encourage
collaboration among students. (I once worked for a visionary principal
who opened a high school with no desks, only tables.) At a Swedish middle school I visited, teachers did not have rooms; students did. Teams
of students would be assigned to certain rooms and teachers would
move in and out of these rooms instead of the students. This, according
to the principal, was an attempt to give the students ownership of that
room, not the teacher.

The learning strategies employed by the teacher encourage, discour-
age, or even prohibit both autonomy in students and a deep understanding of content. When I observe a teacher standing in front of a class for
more than a few minutes, I can be sure that he or she is attempting to
be the "bank of knowledge" and the students are to be passive receivers
of his or her perceived brilliance. The "talking and chalking" teacher is
of little use today and should, therefore, be replaced by the "guide on
the side" teacher who promotes active, collaborative learning in the
classroom. In order to change this role, the teacher, of course, has to be
willing to seemingly give up control of the class. I say "seemingly" because teachers who take on this role and utilize collaborative learning
strategies are still very much in control of the situation. They know exactly what each and every student is doing in their classes. Nancie Atwell, a progressive middle school teacher and author of *In the Middle*
(1987), which was instrumental in my development into a constructivist
teacher, advocates the use of quality management tools in her teaching.
She maintains a clipboard for each class, walking around to each stu-

dent, dialoguing with that student, and taking notes on that student's progress. Atwell also has students maintain folders to be used as reading and writing portfolios so they can return to past work when they or she deems it necessary. The result is a large amount of qualitative data for each child and much more important, I contend, than dozens of meaningless percentage or letter marks in a grade book. Percentages and letter grades really do not tell the student or the parent much about the child's learning. Yet we as parents and teachers have grown so accustomed to these that if they do not appear on a report card, we are upset. We were acculturated by the industrial-age model of schooling where each product is stamped as acceptable (to various degrees: D, C, B, or A) or unacceptable (F). As the Swedish principal stated, we must try not to impose the memories of our schooling onto our children's schooling. Our children deserve an education for the global age, an education of which we were deprived.

Along with teachers, administrators also change roles in the global school. Just as the teacher abstains from giving directives to the students, the principal (and the myriad of assistant principals that American schools employ) will no longer need to direct teachers. Direct supervision will be replaced by personal responsibility. The principal will have the ultimate responsibility for every student and employee's safety and welfare as well as students' learning, but he or she will not need to establish a rule-focused organization in order to do this. Teachers do not need a long list of rules in their classrooms either, if the organization's members accept responsibility. A couple of guidelines developed by the students will suffice.

The need for a great number of administrators at each site will decrease when teachers and students are no longer in need of direct supervision. The principal's main role will be that of facilitating power among the school's stakeholders—the Theory Y leader (see more on Theory Y later in this chapter). It has been said that a great leader is one who seeks to eliminate his or her job. The effective principal in a global-age school will find that he or she needs no help in "administering"—thus, the elimination of the other administrators at the school. But, as noted previously, the principal cannot eliminate his or her job because someone must take ultimate responsibility and someone must act as the spokesperson for the school in both bright and bleak times.

As with the principal, superintendents will see the need to downsize administrative personnel in the central offices. As problems are resolved at the classroom and school level and as curricula are devised individually by every student in collaboration with every teacher, the jobs of most district-level administrators will no longer be necessary. Down will come the layers of bureaucracy that hinder large school districts across the nation, allowing for these organizations to become much more efficient and client friendly. The savings for the districts will be enormous, savings that can be used directly for student learning. It must be noted that noneducators might also wish for school bureaucracies to crumble, but their strategy is to publicize schools' fallacies through irrelevant testing, after which they intend to privatize all schools. This privatization, as I argued earlier, will lead to further polarization of races and social classes. In addition, their methods seem to actually increase bureaucratization of schooling as hundreds, if not thousands, of testing and standards "experts" are now employed at all levels to combat the ESEA mandates. Add in the hundreds of testing and standards consultants that districts and states hire and you can see the bureaucracy begin to "bulge at the seams." So much for "small" government.

RESPONSIBILITY AND INTERNALIZED MOTIVATION

As roles change within the school, students are forced to become responsible for their own learning (as witnessed by their self-developed individual learning plans in Sweden). Class attendance loses importance when the teacher is not responsible for the impossible task of transferring knowledge into the students' heads. I noticed in Sweden that usually half of the students on the class rolls were missing from the classroom, yet the teachers seemed to know where they were: someplace else working on a project or studying collaboratively. As I mentioned previously, two high schools I visited had built several conference rooms so that students could work together without interference from a teacher. This type of conference room is now being discussed in "small schools" reforms as advocated by the ESEA. Yet I doubt that the U.S.

students will ever be left totally unsupervised due to our actual and perceived need to supervise, therefore rendering these rooms useless.

I explained earlier that I asked Swedish high school students why they were so intent upon learning despite not being forced to do so, and they responded that it was their responsibility to learn—a response I found to be quite startling as an American educator. Grades were given only in the high schools, and these did not seem to be great motivators—nor needed to be. Students expressed little concern about what grade they were to receive for each class. Responsibility for learning apparently was internalized by the students.

At a high school in northern Sweden, I observed that much of what progressive American educators had been advocating for over a century was being implemented. At the time, I was a high school assistant principal and was most impressed with the lack of discipline problems at this school of 2,000 sixteen- to nineteen-year-olds. Although I have noted this earlier, I believe it warrants further mention due to its potential impact on U.S. teachers: when I asked teachers about classroom management problems, they looked at me with blank stares. I had to rephrase my question to "What do you do with students who don't do as you ask?" Their replies were "Why wouldn't they?" or even more puzzling to me, "Why would I need to ask them to do something?" Finding unsupervised students in a student lounge, I inquired why they were at school instead of home sleeping or downtown sitting in coffee shops (as I was told is a favorite Swedish teenage pastime). They answered to the effect that it was their responsibility to learn and that they had a better chance of learning when they were at school, not somewhere else. I began to pose this same question to many other students who were not in classes, but were unsupervised in the glassed-in conference rooms, computer labs, or electronics laboratories, among other places on campus, working collaboratively or independently on projects. Their general response was the same as the teenagers in the lounge: it is their responsibility to learn.

I have experienced a bit of jealousy that Swedish schools can foster this type of responsibility and we Americans cannot, but initially what I felt was disbelief that adults trusted teenagers enough to allow them to be unsupervised (student supervision was my main concern as a school administrator, not student learning). And why was there no need for teachers to look over their shoulders or to prod the students to learn? Why did the students respond in such a responsible manner? I wildly theorized that Swedish adolescents matured faster than their American counterparts—maybe something in their diet? My mind brainstormed other absurd ideas, never reaching any seemingly plausible explanations.

Toward the end of my initial stay in Sweden, I met with about twenty other American educators, many of them principals, to develop a report of what we saw in the Swedish schools (the others had visited a dozen schools throughout the country). Regardless of whether my American colleagues visited a high school, a middle school, elementary, adult, or technical school, the reports were the same: teachers trusted students and students accepted the responsibility to learn.

I returned to Sweden twice more to visit other schools in other communities to see if what we had witnessed was a fluke. Indeed, it was not. By design—that is, national curricula—Swedish schools are empowering organizations, empowering teachers as well as students. Although I was impressed with what I saw and the data I collected in my studies, what I witnessed was not novel. In fact, everything I witnessed can be found in American schools, just not all in the same school and surely not all in the same district, let alone statewide! The Swedes had taken American and other educators' ideas, going all the way back to John Dewey, and had apparently implemented them nationwide, which would be the equivalent of Americans implementing these throughout one state—still a commendable achievement.

With autonomy comes responsibility, but autonomy cannot be realized without those in power trusting others. Students will not become responsible for their learning and their behavior unless they believe that they are trusted to do what is right and are supported with a sincere sharing of power. Otherwise, they will see education as something that is done to them, not for them. A change in teaching strategies and learning environments, as are appropriate for constructivist practices, as well as a change of roles in the schools will be necessary for schools to expect students to be responsible for their learning and, thus, responsible citizens. Those who are stuck in an industrial-age organization that is floundering in the global age, as are our schools, subconsciously realize that something is amiss. The result is an internal unrest that often results in outward behavior that does not appear appropriate or explainable. I believe students sense that their schools are not suitable vehicles to carry them to success in this new age. Schooling has lost its relevance. With this sense of inappropriateness, students see schools for what they are: industrial-age relics that are unable to prepare them for their futures. It is no wonder that teachers complain about discipline in the classroom; students rightfully feel that what they are experiencing (or enduring) in the schools is too often a waste of time.

Character education, a greatly debated topic in the United States for over two decades, is an avenue used by some American educators to attempt to instill values in students, values such as responsibility. Cognitive and academic skills are relatively easy to address in U.S. schools as compared to character development. Often the question is "Whose ethics, morals, and values should be instilled in our youth?" Media-hyped instances of school violence and the growing concern of insubordination toward teachers leaves U.S. education in a position where it can no longer keep relegating character education to the background, behind the all-consuming movement to increase standardized test scores. Character is truly part of everything we do in our lives and has much to do with taking responsibility for our own actions. The Swedes understood this and made character development the central theme of their national curricula. It would behoove us to do the same.

Many American teachers and administrators express their concern that a majority of their students have little or no personal responsibility but, as the Swedish principal suggested to me, without the schools trusting students, personal responsibility will not be gained by the students. This giving of trust runs contrary to American educator's great need for control in the classrooms and schools. The release of this control will be painful for teachers, yet ultimately worthwhile if not crucial. It is contrary to the American school tradition of control of the students and the control of schools by well-intentioned (maybe) yet ill-informed government powers. Without this release, however, trust will never be gained and, therefore, neither will responsibility.

CREATING AND SUSTAINING THE
ESSENTIAL VALUE: TRUST

Student responsibility cannot be attained without autonomy, and autonomy cannot be realized without trust. On my second visit to Sweden, I was intent on examining trust in schools, as it seemed to be the missing ingredient for success in American schools, at least from my and my colleagues' views based on our initial visit to Sweden. Before embarking upon this examination, I spent some time studying the element of trust in organizations other than schools (very little literature exists in whole-school trust, which in itself may tell us something about our schools).

To have and hold a democracy where power is shared, a high level of trust must exist among those in power and the general population. In industry, this is trust between management and the workers; in schools, it is a trust between and among administrators, teachers, and students. Trust in individual people within an organization, whether they are co-workers or authority figures, benefits the cooperative nature of the organization. But nearly all trust involves some degree of risk; oftentimes trusting someone can be risky in that the benefits of the trust can be far less than the possible negative outcomes. The result of this risk is the overall confidence one has in the individual in which the trust is placed. A principal who asks teachers to engage in a new, costly reform where success could benefit the students but failure could hurt both the students and the teachers requires a mutually high level of trust between that principal and the school's staff.

The concept of "distrust" can involve acts of revenge, as is seen with recent tragedies where outcast students shoot and kill teachers or other students who had mistreated them in their schools. A breaking of civic order and social identity is a major source of revenge, where people believe that rules and honor are violated and figures of authority abuse their power. Students might feel distrust for a variety of reasons, including the real or perceived instances of teachers or administrators lying to them, showing them disrespect, breaching confidentiality, or not fulfilling promises.

In addition, the aspect of the "abusive authority" (as sometimes demonstrated by the Theory X leader described later in this chapter) or authority figure cruelly treating an underling (such as student) only adds to the perception of distrust and, therefore, a person's desire to seek revenge. Even if a leader or a teacher has earned the trust of an employee or a student, that trust can be broken due to maltreatment, be it continuous or a one-time instance. An absence of trust, not to be confused with distrust, is simply a lack of knowledge of the other. It takes time and socialization to build trust among people in an organization. It can take only an instant for this trust to be irrevocably broken.

Many social scientists believe that trust is the element that makes work in organizations possible and is seen by management experts as essential for managerial success. Trust moderates between and among key organizational behaviors that prove essential to the success of an organization. Education has made limited attempts to implement more flexible organizations over the past few decades, organizations that reflect what industry research suggests is effective. Communication, a key ingredient to organization success, is greatly enhanced by increased trust, through increased openness throughout the organization.

The level of trust in an organization can predict a major decision's effect, whether or not the input of major stakeholders was utilized in making that decision. A person's trust is greatly affected by whether the decision affects him or her personally (individualist) or the group in which he or she most closely identifies within the organization (collectivist). Trust is paramount to collaborative efforts in organizations and is a crucial element in all organizations in the global era.

If schools reorganize themselves into more collaborative structures such as learning communities, the need for trust will increase. Collaboration for teachers, as well as students, will need to be at both the cooperative and assertive levels. If decision making is to be shared, then trust must be increased and strengthened. What this means to education is that if such movements as site-based management (where decision making is shared by those whom the decisions most affect) are to succeed, then trust in the overall organization (school system) must increase.

Getting people to cooperate is often difficult in an individualist culture and is greatly dependent upon how strongly people believe their act will be reciprocated. Those who are cooperating take on the burden of the cooperation while everyone in the group benefits—even those who choose not to cooperate. If this were to continue, cooperation would discontinue. Thus, cooperation depends on participation of all in the organization, not just in isolated instances. Trust also depends on people's beliefs that others will reciprocate cooperative actions.

Trust can be easily lost through inconsistent behaviors. Trust of people in authority has fallen in the United States for the past few decades. This might be attributed in part to the Vietnam War debacle and to Watergate, or "Iran/Contra-gate," or "Monica-gate." It might also be attributed to misunderstanding and confusion about the world in which we now live. Most of us are unable to understand the requirements of living in the global age, assuming we even comprehend that we are no longer in the industrial age! When one party acts in such a way that trust is violated, then trust is lost and cannot easily be regained. Anger, hurt, fear, and frustration only strengthen distrust and may retard or even prohibit the development of trust.

Loss of trust and distrust are not permanent, however, as trust can be regained if considered through its cognitive and emotional components. It takes a high level of commitment from all parties to repair trust, commitment to time and devotion to the resultant resurgence of trust, but is it worth the effort to regain? It must first be recognized that a violation of trust has occurred and what caused this violation. Next, the parties must be willing to admit that the action was destructive and be willing to accept responsibility. Finally, the victim must be willing to forgive and be open to trust once again. Will the disempowered, who have been disenfranchised in our society due in part to the archaic school system, ever again trust schools to prepare them for the future? We educators have our work cut out for us.

COMMUNITIES OF LEARNING: BUILDING TRUST

Collaboration among students is essential if they are to be expected to work in a team setting, a requirement of the global workforce. Most American schooling, as I have noted consistently throughout this book, is very competitive and individualist in structure, curriculum, and nature. This section examines an aspect of schooling that will promote the ideals of a global economy as well as global citizenship.

School size is, with the exception of SES, the best predictor of a child's academic success and is finally being recognized nationally by its inclusion in the ESEA and supported by grants through the Gates Foundation as well as the U.S. Department of Education. After presenting my argument, I describe an alternative to simply destroying all our giant school complexes built for the industrial age or the expensive construction of small schools that are more conducive to effective learning. I realize that we cannot afford a great reconstruction of schools in this time of financial instability brought about, ironically, by our inability to come to grips with globalization. The alternative to massive construction projects is the "learning community" or "school within a school" that reshapes large, impersonal schools into a series of smaller, caring, and effective learning environments.

School Size

The topic of school size is important to those interested in building learning communities because these communities divide large schools into smaller, nearly autonomous schools. As education tries to reform, many ideas have come forth concerning possible models for schools to use. Historically, many citizens and teachers' unions have advocated reducing class size and the size of the school itself. Others, however, cite the lack of research on the costly tactic of reducing classroom and school size when turning down legislation to do just that. Enough evidence now exists to support the establishment of smaller school communities, evidence that has not gone unnoticed by supporters of the ESEA. A synthesis of the research pertaining to school size (Raywid 1998) is quite compelling:

- Students from small schools are more likely to pass major subjects, especially reading and math
- Disadvantaged students in small schools outperform those in large schools
- The impact of size appears to hold across all grade levels and age of students
- School size has more influence on student performance than any other factor that is controllable by the school

The fact that it is the only factor controllable by educators would indicate that it is something that cannot be overlooked and should, in my opinion, be adopted universally.

The impact on the disadvantaged could be the most important aspect of reducing school size (Oxley 1994; Cotton 1996). Although middle class students have actually shown more success in larger schools, all recent research indicates that larger schools are devastating to the disadvantaged. The success of the "advantaged" students could result from the proliferation of giant, middle class, suburban schools. Disadvantaged students in smaller schools cannot easily become "lost in the crowd," or disenfranchised as they might be in a large school. I contend students who are from a disempowered culture also need more attention and resources to overcome the scars made by the inequities in our society.

Another positive aspect of smaller schools is the relative lack of violence as compared to larger schools (Cotton 1996; Raywid 1998). Students in small schools are generally better behaved, tend to drop out at a reduced rate, and have fewer gang-related problems per capita. Much of society's focus in recent years is on the perceived lack of safety due to violence in the nation's schools, a perception fueled by the media. Schools, I believe, have a problem with public relations, as witnessed by recent surveys that give the nation's schools lower grades than local schools. It would greatly benefit the fostering of positive public relations if schools were to show significant declines in violence—and violence can be reduced by limiting the size of schools. With an improved public opinion of schooling may come more public support, both moral and financial.

While it is debatable how "small is small" and how "big is big," we can safely assume that the prison-like monstrosities constructed in the past several decades are detrimental to learning. Some scholars believe that 400–800 students (Cotton 1996) are optimal while others would support schools with not more than 200–225 students (Shapiro, Benjamin, and Hunt 1995). Today, some metropolitan school districts have high schools as large as 5,000, while 2,000 to 3,000 is not uncommon. Typically, the largest schools in the largest school districts in the most populous states do the worst academically. Most socioeconomically disadvantaged students are found in these larger schools and, conversely, it is this sector of the student population that is the most positively affected by small schools.

The learning community or schools-within-schools concept, as will be described in the next section, attempts to do more than simply raise grades of students; it also endeavors to develop better people to help create a better society for all. The small school seems to have a favorable impact on students in many nonacademic aspects of their lives. Participation per capita in extracurricular activities increases in a small school, allowing the students to become more involved in their school organization (Cotton 1996). This is attributed to the need in small schools for everyone's involvement (including parents) in order for extracurricular activities to be possible. In addition, tobacco, alcohol, and drug use are decreased in small schools (Raywid 1998). Post–high school behaviors such as an increase in matriculation into college are also attributed to students attending small schools (Raywid 1998). Despite all the advantages of small schools, we continue to build massive schools because small schools are deemed to be economically inefficient to build and sustain. Using our factory mind-sets, we insist that bigger is better and more economical. We shop at "mega-marts" where items are sold in mass quantities that provide lower costs to the consumer. This model cannot be transferred to schooling because "mega-schooling" is detrimental to our children. They are not mass-produced widgets; they are social beings who need time and care to properly develop as learners, citizens, and caring members of society. The immediate expenses of building small schools can be overcome by the long-term rewards: improved learning and better global citizens.

Schools within Schools

Until smaller schools can be built, it is much more pragmatic to restructure a larger school into a cluster of smaller ones, or "schools within schools." Schools within schools should prove to be a much more economically viable solution to the problems caused by existing large schools. Transforming a large school into a cluster of smaller ones would be the only economically feasible alternative to building smaller schools. Again, the Swedes are ahead of the curve—the Swedish Education Act of 1994 called for each municipality to provide sixteen career-based programs in their upper secondary schools. These programs essentially act as schools within schools in that students stay within a program for their years in upper secondary school and share the same group of teachers.

Teachers are assigned, or choose, to be in one program and work collaboratively to meet the needs of their program's students.

American schools would indeed be wise to adopt career-focused programs such as those offered in Sweden. Students could choose from a variety of communities within their school, communities whose curricula are centered on career orientations or areas of personal interest. For instance, the Swedes have a music program where all the students in the program learn math, science, social studies, English, and Swedish all from teachers within the music program. The binding element to all of those classes is music, and whether the students are actual musicians, singers, or simply listeners to music, they are motivated to learn because all content is connected to music and all students and teachers that are in the program share a love for music. The business aspects of music are also learned in the program: producing, recording, and marketing. In the United States, I can envision such a program becoming so large in a suburban or urban high school that it would need to split into two or more programs. Student and teacher motivation, if the program were planned and implemented correctly, would be exceptional. The bonding that would take place would allow teachers and students to know each other well enough so that they could understand each person's learning, social, and emotional needs. It is not the intent of the programs to simply develop musicians, for example, or those who can earn a living in the music industry; the programs hope to transfer the emotional commitment that each student has for music into learning of the other subjects, that is, motivate students to learn.

Other programs in U.S. high schools could be social sciences (branching into law, psychology, social work, or teaching), health, engineering (electrical, mechanical, or chemical), transportation (automobiles, boats, airplanes), food sciences, and hospitality, just to name a few. I can imagine that all would have, at the high school level, basic outcomes from state or national levels, outcomes that would be assessed through performance, not a pencil-and-paper test. The basic curricula for all programs could be set by state or national entities, but could be molded to fit the needs at the local level. The Swedes divided the subject areas into levels so that universities and employers would be able to understand a student's knowledge based on the level of, for example, math he or she took and passed. There would, for instance, be a minimum level of math that must be mastered for every program. Obviously, those in the engineering programs would be expected to reach a higher level of math than, for example, social sciences. Unlike the two Swedish programs that were in my estimation college preparatory, it would be of the utmost importance for schools and districts to ensure that all learning communities give their students equal opportunity to be prepared for university. Essentially, the reasons for creating learning communities are to (1) motivate students to learn, (2) connect schooling with its environment, and most important, (3) create smaller, nurturing, family-like communities where all feel valued.

Swedish students deciding that they do not like or are not suited to a certain program are allowed to change programs, usually after the first year. This keeps them from skipping back and forth from one area to the other, never quite accomplishing the requirements of any one program. Also, it would be nearly impossible for each and every one of the 14,000-plus U.S. school districts to offer all the available programs. Cooperative agreements between and among districts as well as distance learning would be necessary, especially in rural areas. Once again, the basic premises of offering career-focused programs are motivation and relevance. Without these two, we can do nothing but continue to force students to come to school and coerce them to learn, both of which are proven failures. The schools-within-schools model allows for everyone in the organization to learn, a crucial aspect if the organization is to continue to grow and stay flexible to meet the needs of its environment.

The Learning Organization

According to Peter Senge in his best-selling management book *The Fifth Discipline* (1990), organizations cannot afford to have one mastermind dictating to others through layers of bureaucracy what needs to be done in order for that organization to be successful. Despite our seemingly desperate need for hero worship, everyone in an organization must share responsibility in the global age. In addition to sharing responsibility in the actual work taking place, Senge advocates that all must participate in a continuous cycle of learning, becoming "symbolic analysts" if an organization is to succeed in the third wave, because those who cannot continue to learn and adapt will quickly be discarded or cause the entire organization to fail. Communication, preferably dialogue, is the key to such a learning organization. This dialoguing differs greatly from a mere discussion in that it is not competitive; all are enticed to become involved instead of a few who monopolize the talk, as is too often the case when a subordinate engages in discussion with his or her boss.

Borrowing much from Senge's flexible, ever-growing learning organization is the concept of the learning community in the school (or vice versa—I am not sure which came first, the learning organization or the learning community; it may be a case of parallel innovations). Learning is change, and working with and initiating change are essential elements of learning organizations and properly planned and implemented learning communities. Some U.S. school districts are utilizing learning communities, as are the high school programs in Sweden. This utilization may ensure that our children will be able to excel in the changing world described by Alvin Toffler, Senge, and globalization scholars.

The formation of teams of workers is essential in the development of a learning organization. The "middle school concept" calls for teachers to work in interdisciplinary teams with a group of 90 to 150 students. I worked in such a structure at three different schools, as a teacher and then as an administrator. The benefits were obvious. As a teacher, I collaborated with three or four other teachers who shared my students. We planned together and discussed our students' concerns as a cohesive team. As an administrator, I found that most student concerns were resolved within the team of teachers; it was not my job to step in to resolve small problems, but to lend support to the teachers to help them resolve problems themselves. This is exactly the kind of support teachers should be giving students so that they are able to resolve conflict on their own in a society that values responsibility.

The middle school model is widespread throughout the United States, but the concept is not. Many middle schools—and I worked in one—are simply junior high schools in that they do not embrace the middle school concept of caring and support. They act as places of control and punishment, where the students resent the teachers and the teachers resent the authority of administrators at all levels. This is a very ugly and uncomfortable environment for both children and adults. It is ripe with distrust and failure, failure to learn and failure to promote a positive work culture. The only reason a factory-style school continues to exist without riotous students (and parents) is through the relentless use of coercive controls. Students can be successful later in life despite this type of school only if they are fortunate enough to have been born into middle- or high-SES households; therefore, students most affected by the industrial-age school model are those in poverty. In essence, the middle school concept of having teachers and students work in teams focuses curricula and teaching strategies around student needs. One day, I hope, it will be realized that these needs include being able to live and work in the global village. The middle school concept and approaches are indeed on the right track.

Educators can learn from successful companies that have adopted the organizational structures and provide opportunities for their workers to attain the traits necessary for survival and success in the global age. Learning communities or schools within schools require more collaboration among students and teachers in smaller, caring environments. Within these communities, democracy tends to be the governance of choice, perhaps due to the high levels of comfort students, teacher, and administrators feel as members of the communities.

INDIVIDUALIZED LEARNING

Factory-model schools are designed to "produce" as many graduates as possible, as efficiently as possible. The quality control experts at the end of the assembly line take the form of standardized tests. These tests, based on the misguided intentions and bolstered by the misinformed media, are to act as a filter to ensure that no student is given a high school diploma for simply going through the motions of schooling, something that *A Nation at Risk* argued was the case in too many high schools. The standards movement intends to establish criteria (i.e., standardized tests) that ensure that no child is "socially promoted"—that is, not able to demonstrate the knowledge required to . . . well, I am not sure exactly what standardized testing establishes. Except, perhaps, that at a given time, a student can demonstrate that he or she is able to answer a certain percentage of questions on a certain test under certain conditions—certainly not enough validity to close down schools or terminate teachers' and administrators' contracts.

Clearly, this system is lacking if our intent is to prepare students for success (not merely survival) in the global economy. And, more important, our system of schooling definitely lacks the ability to ensure the fostering of the global citizen. If we change the structure of schooling to more resemble that of a global organization, we can ensure students will have a better opportunity to learn what is necessary for success in the global village. A learning philosophy exists that promotes the type of schooling that is necessary for the global age, and that is constructivism as described earlier.

Constructivism, which allows for students to build individual meaning from their learning, promotes the type of individualized curricula that are necessary for a society such as ours that is a mix of hundreds of cultures and languages. Each child comes to school with a different set of experiences from his or her culture and environment. The Swedes embraced individualized learning as one of the mandates of the 1994 Education Act, structuring their schools and curricula to reflect constructivism's individualized curricular focus. Valuing the individual's unique background and perspective allows for democracy to flourish. (The current educational buzzword for individualized learning is "differentiated curricula." Knowing this term may be of some benefit to the reader as the term *differentiation* might be thrown around by educators while in the reader's presence.)

When observing teachers who have serious problems with classroom management, I find that one of two situations exists: the teacher is totally unprepared to teach or the teacher is attempting to teach the entire class at the same time—and sometimes both! Lesson preparation is important whether you are a traditional teacher throwing "knowledge" out to the masses or a progressive teacher fostering learning in each and every student. The traditional teacher, however, can get away with faulty plans through sheer intimidation of students and rock-solid control. Of course, students do not learn effectively in this environment, but classroom management concerns are at a minimum (although learning concerns surely exist). If our number one reason for having schools is to keep students off the streets, then this control is appropriate. I firmly believe, however, that it is our moral obligation to prepare children for the future, the global age. An emphasis on control, therefore, is not necessary and is, in fact, detrimental.

What is necessary is the understanding that each student has a unique background and learning needs. Our schools are structured so that thirty or so children in one room will learn fifty minutes' worth of content all at the same speed and to the same degree; then a bell will ring, and they will go on to another room to do the same. This is absurd. Yet, try to explain this to the people propagating the standards movement. "No child left behind?" Left behind what or whom? If we really do not want a child to come through schooling without learning, as *A Nation at Risk* claimed was too often the case, then we need to reexamine what is to be learned and how it is to be learned. Teaching to the masses is a pedagogical disaster.

When a teacher is having difficulties with classroom management and I am somehow able to convince this person that authoritarianism is not conducive to real learning, then I help the teacher devise strategies to divide the class into groups and to adjust the content so that students can learn at their own pace and in their preferred styles. If a student prefers socializing while learning, fine. Allow him or her to learn with others who learn through socialization (by the way, this is the most effective way for most of us to learn). If a child prefers being alone, then it would be beneficial to allow that student to be alone, but do not keep him or her consistently isolated as it is essential that every child gain and use effective social skills. Students will sometimes wish to work independently one day (or minute) and collaboratively another. Fine. Teachers need to adjust to this, and being able to adjust requires the creation of a classroom that is nontraditional, that does not look like the classrooms we had in the industrial age.

Leadership in Global-Age Schools

Creating systems that can operate autonomously may imply that leaders would or could be obsolete. Nothing could be further from the truth. *Traditional* leadership—leadership that closely supervises and directs underlings—would be obsolete. A fluid organization that can change easily to meet the needs of its clients requires that all stakeholders accept some leadership role. No one can expect to be a productive member of a team-oriented organization when he or she does not possess leadership qualities or is unwilling to participate in a leadership role.

Over forty years ago, Douglas McGregor (1960) theorized that essentially all leaders fall into two categories, what he called Theory X and Theory Y. The Theory X leader is the traditional leader who ensures that all workers are closely supervised and accounted for. He (this is, after all, a patriarchal leadership role) dictates what is to be done and when it is to be done. Control is extremely important. Three types of the Theory X leader can be devised based on how the leader accepts input and acts on it. Type 1-X, whom I will call the "bear," does not want nor does he accept input from underlings about anything. He wants to be deemed strong, independent and, perhaps, a maverick. Many people say they enjoy working for such leader because they "know where they stand": there are no gray areas, only black and white. When he makes a decision, you know it will stand. Many of us tend to see this leader as a hero: tough and determined, standing up for what he believes in. Yes, the cowboy.

The 2-X leader graciously asks for input from employees, but then callously ignores this input. He may hold meetings to gather information and opinions, but everyone knows, including the leader, that he has no intention of implementing these ideas. In contrast, a 3-X leader is the "weasel" who requests input, says he is going to implement others' ideas, and then does it his way. Regardless of which type of Theory X leader an organization has, the people know that their input is not valued and, therefore, stop bothering to care. They know their role is to be mere sheep, passive and nonthinking, easily controlled. This is how our students view their roles in U.S. schools and how they are treated.

Theory Y leaders not only solicit opinions from others, she (this is a feminine leadership style) insists on it. Unlike the weasel, she is determined to legitimize her employee's ideas by implementing them—even if they often run counter to her beliefs. She believes that a wrong decision is sometimes less destructive than not confirming her coworkers' importance. The Theory Y leader will lead global organizations because she (let us hope that men are capable of leading this way, also) will not allow pride or status to prevent her from disseminating power and, thus, motivating employees and other stakeholders to participate in the direction of the organization. (Although Theory Y is indeed a feminine style, I have worked for and with several female Theory X supervisors who act in the same manner as male Theory X supervisors.)

How would Theory Y leadership look in a school? A fully flexible school organization would need only one "top" leader and that would be the principal. Someone, as I mentioned previously, has to take final responsibility. Team members in various learning communities would all have leadership positions and would share in the credit when results are good and in the responsibility if things go awry. The principal, however, would be the master facilitator, ensuring that the school operates in the best interests of the stakeholders. If something goes wrong, no matter who is at fault, the principal must ensure the problem is resolved, either by herself or by someone else. The same can be said of the superintendent, but on a much broader scale. The superintendent would depend on the principals to operate their schools so that all stakeholders learn, but must be completely responsible if they do not. Still, the superintendent must trust the principals enough not to micromanage them, just as the superintendent would not want to be micromanaged by the school board.

CONSIDERING PERSONALITY TYPES FOR LEADERSHIP AND CHANGE

Can anyone be a Theory Y leader? Do all workers enjoy having this type of leader? In an attempt to answer these questions, I turn to personality studies. A vast amount of research has been conducted involving the Myers-Briggs Type Indicator (MBTI) over the past half-century (Myers and Myers 1995). In addition, over one million people in the United States alone have taken this personality test since its first publication during World War II. Because of the sheer volume of research and the number of those who have taken this test, I find it desirable to use the MBTI in discussing personalities and leadership.

The MBTI measures sixteen different personality types, lumped into four separate "temperaments." Each generally describes a person's preferences for action and thought. Its developers, Isabel Briggs-Myers and her mother, Katherine Cook Briggs, readily admit that no one consistently acts as his or her temperament indicates he or she should nor do they predict he or she would; however, nearly everyone taking the test can easily be categorized into a single temperament. No one is exactly like the description of a single temperament; usually a person has some qualities of all four. However, the instrument has been found to be valid when used for employment placements. Certain characteristics of those who test out in a single temperament are inclined toward certain jobs or professions. In addition to aiding in career choice and placement, this categorization allows us to gain a better understanding of those within our organization. I will use the MBTI in an attempt to explain why certain leadership styles are found in schools and why these styles are allowed to remain in power.

What is of the utmost importance in the discussion of leadership in schools is the percentage of each of the four temperaments who decide to teach or act as a school administrator as compared to the percentages found in the general public. Approximately 55 percent of school personnel are of the temperament (Sensing-Judging or "SJ") that prefers orderliness and predictability. People with this temperament tend to eschew change and often look to the past as "the good old days." Only about 38 percent of the general population is of this temperament, which obviously means there is an overrepresentation of SJs in schools (Keirsey and Bates 1984). An overdependence on rules and regulations can lead to direct and indirect opposition to school reform, unless the reform is based on past methods and beliefs such as those reforms advocated by the standards movement. An SJ leader would be one who dictates policy and expects rigid conformity, likely a Theory X-1 leader. SJ teachers are happy to follow directives (although they still may complain about them) and would be uncomfortable with having to make decisions they feel should be left to their superiors. I like to refer to the SJ leader as the "wolf" and the SJ follower as the "sheep." The sheep, when put into a position of authority, such as teaching a class of students, easily morphs into the wolf. Military-like regimentation is expected of each and every child. The factory model of schooling is a perfect fit for both the sheep and the wolf as it provides predictability and precision—at least in theory. I have established that this type of schooling is not conducive to the fostering of the global citizen, one who can understand and adapt to change. The SJ resists change at every opportunity.

Schools primarily consist of only two of the four temperaments: the SJ and the NF (Intuitive-Feeling). The NFs are able to examine the "big picture" of situations, something the SJs cannot or will not do, yet the NFs have a tendency to "think with their hearts" rather than analyze situations. Only 12 percent of the general population is NF, so this temperament is also overrepresented in the schools. NFs rarely make it into leadership positions in schools, as only about 20 percent of school administrators are of this temperament (Keirsey and Bates 1984). With the majority of school leaders being SJs, the factory-model school's desire to have a more controlled structure—a Theory X leader and a staff of sheep—prevails. By the way, Intuitive-Thinkers (NT) and Sensing-Perceiving (SP) make up only a combined 8 percent of school personnel as compared to one-half of the general population. The NT is referred to as the "little scientist," constantly seeking exposure to intellectual pursuits, something lacking greatly in the factory-model school. Those who seek excitement and constant change are of the SP temperament (Keirsey and Bates 1984). The second-wave school provides neither excitement nor change, only mundane, predictable tasks and rigid adherence to rigid policy. Therefore, there is nothing in our schools that would entice an SP.

The NFs in schools, though a minority, are the most vocal. They are compassionate about their students and humankind, in general, sometimes to a fault. NFs strongly support the democratic process and are deeply interested in the needs of others (Keirsey and Bates 1984). This temperament would be an excellent fit for a global school. It is the factory-style school and school system that keeps them out of leadership positions, as they are deemed too soft on students and others (teachers) whom they would supervise. If the NTs were available to lead schools (they are not, as the traditional school structure is not logical to them), they would do so scientifically. Change would be logical, based on sound theory and research. I am confident the NT would insist upon school reforms for the global age, and would not care if he or she upset any of the underlings, as logic takes precedence over others' feelings. The SPs are more likely to come and go quickly in schools, not staying around long enough to assume a leadership position. Their need for excitement and change may be the catalyst for much-needed school reform. The system as it is, however, spurns people with this temperament because they are the true risk-takers in our society. Indeed, no risks need to be taken if we want schools to remain the same or steered backward toward the mythical glory days of our past.

The indicator "N" or Intuitive is an interesting study, one that I feel compelled to share with the reader. N's make up less than a quarter of the population, yet about 75 percent of corporate executives are intuitive (Myers and Myers 1995). Two main differences exist between an N and its counter, S: their view of the world in terms of scope, and their ability to use evidence to see reality. The N has a very broad view of a situation, an organization, and the world, in general; contrastingly, the S sees with "blinders." Sensing individuals are more interested in minute detail and are challenged to see beyond the parts of the whole, whereas the Intuitive individual sees the whole more than the parts. S's have great difficulty comprehending that which they cannot sense: see, touch, hear, smell, feel. The lack of physical evidence does not deter the N, as he or she seems to understand what is not sensed physically (Myers and Myers 1995). The high percentage of Intuitives in leadership positions in innovative organizations and the lack of N's in school leadership frightens me—yet explains much of our present situation. Business organizations need to meet the needs of their clients or they simply go out of business, losing market share to those organizations that can. Schools, however, have no real competition to compel them to change (at least not progressive change), nor do they have an intuitive leadership that sees the need for this change. With the system of schooling as it is, and with the stranglehold the standards movement has on education, it is unlikely that the N leader will be common any time soon.

I do not, however, want to be on record as saying SJs are not important members of an organization. They are very strong in organizational skills, keeping other temperaments on track. Their strengths need to be used wisely while keeping their desires for control and predictability from interfering with the development of the global school. It is the overabundance of SJs in schools that could be hindering real school change, a hindrance that has led to the culture of distrust and accountability movement. Keirsey and Bates in their analysis of MBTI temperaments, *Please Understand Me* (1984), say that traditional schools were made by SJs for SJs. I concur.

As school structures become more organic and flatter, teaming will also be an essential component. The struggle between the NFs and the SJs continue in the team setting. SJs will continue to argue for the status quo because it is known and comfortable. As they greatly outnumber all other temperaments in a school, they will need to be catered to. To institute change, schools will need to know and understand SJs' desires in working in team settings. According to Jean Kummerow, Nancy Barger, and Linda Kirby in *Work Types* (1997, 136–37), some of these are:

- Specific communication that is concrete, clear, and concise
- Full information about issues that are relevant to them (will affect them)
- Decision making, to include collection and use of relevant data, that is made quickly, firmly, precisely, and with finality (they despise ambiguity)
- Knowledge of who is in charge and how decisions will be made
- Conflicts that are defined clearly and concretely
- Feedback about specific behaviors, with general comments about performance to include real examples
- An up-front agreement to meet deadlines and follow through, with clear consequences

The NFs, the only other significant temperament in the schools, also have their own desires in the workplace. Some of them are:

- Communication that focuses on the overall plan and general issues, rather than details of everyone's work and contains a personal connection with recognition of them as an individual
- Decision making to include recognition of wider ramifications and consideration of connections
- Feedback that assesses overall patterns, with general comments about their impact
- The resolution of personal issues before proceeding with a task

- Leadership that is interested in all individuals and includes every-one's opinions

It is obvious that the two have little in common as far as perceptions of good leadership and effective workplace environments. This demonstrates the great internal struggles schools face in attempting change. A leader would need to possess an ability to meet the desires of all those "at the table." The NFs' strengths are that they favor personal connections, which would allow them to avoid personal conflicts in a team, conflicts that can destroy a team's work. They can, however, get caught up in their feelings and those of others in the group, which could force them to lose focus on the goals. NFs, to their credit, have a "big-picture" view of the world that would allow them to understand the vision of the school, the long-term plans, and how each decision affects or is affected by the vision and long-term plans.

While it appears that SJs prefer to have someone who is strong, decisive, and dictates what others should do (Theory X leader), the SJs can be convinced that the goal of the school and the change involved is worthwhile. One way to do this involves concrete planning. Although it is essential that all plans be flexible, they can still appear solid—they can solidly plan for flexibility. Plans, for instance, could include everyone's input, something that would typically make the SJ conclude that the plans are "fluff" and the leader is weak. But if in the plans it is demanded that all give their input, the SJs might comply. It is, obviously, a command with which they must comply. Those in leadership positions can also persuade the SJs by setting deadlines and following through with them. The real "trick" of the global leader, especially in schools dominated by SJs, is to keep the appearance of running a "tight ship" while allowing for flexibility. This is not an easy task to accomplish. If the SJ feels that the leader is compromising the structure of the organization by being too willing to change, they may refute both the leader and the vision.

SJs keep the Theory X leader in power and, therefore, ensure the proliferation of bureaucracies. They also endorse the typical American hero. They have a need to be led and seek a powerful person to lead them. The Theory Y leader, who has the skills necessary to develop and sustain the organic global organization, needs to "shapeshift" himself or herself into the hero desired by the SJs. In industry, TQM is often forced from above: either accept it or get out. Although this is the antithesis of quality management, it often works because those who have existed in an industrial-age organization are often comfortable with the status quo and indeed need to be forced to change. This forcing, at least as far as schools are concerned, should only be a temporary "kick start" or the internal motivation necessary for the global organization will never be allowed to develop. Teachers who are accustomed to being told what to do will need to be able to learn to make decisions for themselves just as they must allow students to do the same. It is difficult, if not impossible, for teachers who insist on having an authority figure tell them what to do to establish learning environments where students become personably responsible.

Although the developers of the MBTI contend that temperaments are inherent and the preferences that come with them are not changeable, we educators must find ways to make change in global schools possible while still working with the SJ. The resistance to change from NFs will be slight; they only need to be shown the vision and believe that they and their students' personal needs will be met. That is easily done. The SJ, on the other hand, will be much more of a challenge. One can predict that with the change of schooling for the global age, fewer and fewer SJs will desire to work in schools. Schools that are less rigid and more ambiguous, meeting the individual needs of the students rather than conforming to policy and following procedures, may repel SJs. It is hoped that the two "missing" temperaments, the NT and the SP, will find schools to be more inviting. The contributions that these two temperaments can make to schools would be tremendous. The SP, for instance, desires change; the global organization must be ever changing to meet its ever-changing environment. Change, as well as the general success of the organization, is dependent on empirical research and its subsequent data, something that greatly interests the NT and something in which he or she excels. The absence of these two temperaments in the schools could explain much of the failure of schools to be relevant in the global age.

STARTING EARLY

Something that impressed me from my observations in Sweden was the Swedes' focus on their youngest children. The Skolverket and Swedish law provide child care for all children between ages one and twelve (from birth to at least twelve months, the child's mother or father must be allowed parental leave). Nearly two-thirds of all children between one and five attend a preschool that is designed to prepare them for compulsory school, which typically begins for children at age seven. Each of the 278 municipalities must provide preschools that are divided into groups of fifteen to twenty children, with a minimum of three adults for each group. Of the adults assigned to the groups, over one-half have university degrees in preschool education, and nearly all have at least some formal education in early childhood. In addition, a government home-care program is available where "childminders" provide care at their home. Nearly three-fourths of all children ages one to five participate in a government-supported preschool. The cost for any preschool service is never to exceed 3 percent of the household income. Before- and after-school care for children up to age twelve are provided in "leisure-time centers," which 62 percent of children aged six to nine attend. These are staffed by personnel who generally have university degrees in recreational studies. All university-educated preschool and leisure-time personnel earn salaries comparable to compulsory school-teachers; even the less-educated "day care attendant" earns a monthly wage that is about 75 percent of what an elementary teacher in Sweden typically earns. All these measures ensure that Swedish children are cared for by trained providers and that all parents can afford to have these services (Skolverket 2001). The Swedes truly believe that no child should be left behind. U.S. politicians need to take note.

In the Swedish preschools, as in all their public schools, the values of democracy, trust, and responsibility are paramount. The national curriculum for preschool is almost identical to those of the compulsory and noncompulsory/adult schools in that they promote values over academics. Teachers of four-year-olds described to me how they strove to have their students participate in decision making. One time, they explained, the students in two classes of about twenty each were convinced that they should all go on a field trip to a nearby park, ostensibly to learn as

well as play. The teachers found this undesirable as the weather was bad
and it is, quite frankly, a lot of work taking students to a park. The students won out, according to the teachers, because it was a decision that
they were encouraged to make and they were indeed adamant about
the field trip. The teachers, of course, could have vetoed the students'
decision, but at what cost? They said that if they refused to take them to
the park, the students would have seen that their opinions were not valid.

As an American, I would think that students cannot make many decisions because their judgment is not mature enough, especially at age
four. But why not make that a goal in U.S. schools, that all students will
be *capable* of making all decisions and given the power to do so? By
necessity, preschool teachers must take on a different role than they do
now in the United States, one that nurtures decision-making abilities
and maturity. With maturity comes responsibility and vice versa. By not
allowing our children, at the earliest opportunities, to make responsible
decisions, and by not fostering their abilities to do so, we are promoting
a culture of helplessness. A democracy depends on mature decisions
made by all, and these decisions need to be made by those who can and
do make informed decisions, using information that is gathered in many
forms from many references, not merely spoon-fed simplistic knowledge, for which they are too often tested in our age of accountability.

Although I advocate for formal education of our children to begin as
early as possible, I also promote a system of paid leave that allows parents to bond with their babies and toddlers so that the children's basic
emotional needs can be met. This will require, of course, a commitment
to the institution of parenthood from industry (to allow for such) and
from different levels of government (to enforce such). Nationally ac-
credited preschools should be provided at no or minimal cost to parents,
beginning with one-year-olds. These schools must be staffed by educated and licensed teachers, not baby-sitters—teachers who are willing
and able to nurture children to become thinking, mature citizens, who
are themselves capable and willing to take on the responsibility of main-
taining a democracy. A model for this preschool curriculum and learning
strategies has existed for decades throughout our nation as well as much
of the world: Montessori schools. This system of schooling is reflected
in the Swedish preschool I studied and warrants an explanation of what
it is and how it can help promote global schooling in the United States

Montessori and Global-Age Schooling

Maria Montessori, trained as a biologist and Italy's first female physician, opened her first school in 1907 in Rome. The school and its curriculum were built around Montessori's belief that children should not be coerced into learning, but instead allowed to discover knowledge at their own pace in an environment conducive to exploration. Developmental stages, influential to Jean Piaget's work, and communal learning environments were the core of her Rome school and the hundreds of schools that have followed this model over the past century (Loeffler 2002).

According to the Montessori model, schools must create what Montessori called "prepared environments" that maintained the "normal" development for each child. Each child is unique and must interact with these environments to find his or her own way through the stages of learning, social, and physical development. The "whole child" must develop rather than simply the quantitative and communication (especially reading and writing) that are the most significant foci of American education, as evidenced by what is supposedly assessed on high-stakes tests. Montessori surmised that all parts of the child's life are connected and must be allowed to progress naturally with guidance from educators (Powell 2000). This links to the multiple intelligences theory of Howard Gardner (1999), who advocates the need to address nine intelligences found within each person (e.g., musical, spatial, kinetic) to go along with the traditional intelligences (math and language) catered to in our schools. Traditionalists seem to approve of music education, physical education, art education, dance, and so forth as long as these do not take away from the basics. Gardner says, and Montessori would agree, that people learn though different avenues. The whole person must be considered if we are to ensure that all children are to learn to their highest potential. This coincides with the Swedish model of schools within schools that are focused on career or interests so that students learn within the context of what interests them.

As noted above, the Montessori school model resembles the Swedish preschool I visited. Prepared environments were used to promote the core values of Montessori—responsibility, autonomy, spirituality, cooperation, and community—all with a focus on independence from adult control. I do not pretend to be a scholar on preschool education in the United States or abroad, but I have my doubts as to whether these values are emphasized in typical American preschools. If they were, then most of our concerns in the later schooling years would diminish, if not completely vanish. It is not difficult to see the similarities between the core values that I advocate in our schools, what the Swedish curricula focus upon, and those on which the Montessori schools base their curriculum.

The roles of teachers in Montessori schools are similar to what I observed at all levels in Swedish schools, that is, they are mediators of knowledge: conduits between the content and the student versus the traditional U.S. teacher who is the fount of knowledge and the transmitter of it (Powell 2000). If students are to truly discover knowledge for themselves, then the teacher must be more of a guide (yes, a facilitator) rather than a controlling knowledge czar. What I find interesting in the Montessori model is that there is a high level of control by the teacher in regard to the learning environment. Much time and effort is put into preparing the environment for each child. I found this true as I tried constructivist practices as a middle school teacher. My planning time probably tripled and my time in the classrooms became more exhausting as I seemed to be doing more work, at least initially. After a few months, I became comfortable with my new role in the class (yes, as a facilitator) and found that my work was not as exhausting as when I tried to control all thirty-five students in each of my classes, attempting to have each child learn the same thing at the same time. My transformation into a constructivist teacher was much the same as what the Swedish teachers said they experienced: it was labor-intensive in the beginning because of the tremendous planning involved as well as frustrating to change the way I conducted my classroom. I agree with the Swedes that this was indeed worthwhile, as my students were more engaged and motivated to learn when I acted as a learning promoter rather than classroom dictator.

Montessori schooling complements and augments constructivism in many ways. For instance, both contend that the learning experiences of each child are unique and that these experiences should be nurtured and fostered by the schools and the adults in the schools (Powell 2000). It does, however, differ significantly from another model of schooling that I find extremely interesting: the Sudbury Valley Model of Schooling (see Greenberg 1992). Sudbury Valley schools, like Montessori schools, are found worldwide and seem to be based on the constructivist and Montessori beliefs that each child is a unique learner who must learn at his or her own pace; at Sudbury Valley schools, however, children are allowed free rein to study what and when they want. The environment is sheer freedom. If the student does not want to learn "constructively" (according to what a traditionalist or even I would consider as such) on a certain day or many days in a row, then that is his or her right. The premise is that natural curiosity, left unfettered, will compel the child to learn on his or her own through exploration or from peers or adults. If the child chooses to play instead of engage in what appears to be learning, then so be it. The argument is that much (if not most) of what can be learned by a child is learned through play. Promoters of the Sudbury Valley schooling model argue that it is highly successful with most children, adolescents, and teenagers; and their evidence is quite compelling—although I would not even dream of advocating this model in today's political environment.

Montessori schooling can be found beyond the preschool ages, but they are most noted for their successes with very young learners. We can learn much from their successes with older students because their theories and practices are sound. I would venture that most American parents eventually take their children out of Montessori schools as, being Americans, they are convinced that the highest levels in public schooling are meant for structured learning of "truths" (the mishmash that passes as important knowledge on standardized tests). The Swedes seemed to use a model that was not dissimilar to that used by Montessori schools and they, in my opinion and from the data provided by the Third International Math and Science Survey (NCES 1999), are very successful in encouraging students to learn "the basics" while still fostering the development of citizens for the global age. The key to restructuring our schooling might indeed lie with how we initiate our children's formal education and, of course, we cannot forget the lessons they and we have learned from this value-laden model of schooling.

EIGHT

Change and Schooling

In chapters 4 and 5, I described two major obstacles facing us as we strive to develop schooling for the global age: (1) power and control issues in the schools as well as in society, and (2) our society's penchant for individualism. I then outlined a national curriculum based on values and a vision for schooling in the new millennium and beyond. I now feel compelled to address two other obstacles that must be overcome if schools and schooling are to prepare students for the global age: (1) changing the way we think about schools and (2) change itself.

Throughout this book, I have referred to a principal in Sweden opening a presentation about schooling for today and tomorrow by asking those in attendance, both educators and community members, to forget about their own experiences in school. Their experiences are no longer relevant to today because they were educated for the industrial age. What numbers of the audience remembered about their education was vastly different from what the schools in that principal's district in central Sweden looked like regarding organization, teaching strategies, curricula, and mind-set about how schooling should be conducted. The same can be said for those of us who have completed our K–12 schooling in the United States; we cannot and should not associate what was done *to* us in schools to what should now be taking place in schools. Unfortunately, with the exception of some new technology, the U.S. schools of today are indeed identical to the schools we, our parents, and our grandparents attended.

"Golden memories" of schools and the schooling process are what we tend to remember as we grow older, much the same as our feelings about old television shows and fashion trends. Our past experiences, when remembered through rose-colored glasses, make us feel warm inside and somehow a bit righteous. What we did and experienced was, in our minds, superior to the present. This is especially true about our schooling experiences. As the world around us keeps changing, usually faster than we can comprehend, it is quite comforting to us that we can go back to our old schools and everything is pretty much the way it was when we left. Only the faces and the clothing styles have changed (unless you went to high school in the 1960s and '70s, as I did—then you would find that many of the high school students today dress as badly as we did). There is something comforting to know that with all of the world's changes, we can count on the schools to be the same.

But they should not be the same, and the fact that they are is criminal. Media and politicians criticize today's schools, saying they are not nearly as good as they used to be. I have heard this from people ranging in age from their early twenties to their eighties. Did schooling deteriorate just in the past five or six years, as the "twenty-somethings" would have us believe? Their criticisms of schools mirror those of the elderly: no discipline, lack of respect for teachers, lazy teachers, and so on. It amazes me to hear someone in his or her mid-twenties telling me that high schools are different from when they were in school. It has now been over a quarter century since I was in high school and I can tell the reader with all honesty that today's schools are nearly identical to when I was a public school student.

I stated in previous chapters that schooling today is better than it ever has been—that is, as far as teaching basic skills to as many as possible. The "good old days" were not so good. The dropout rate was over 50 percent until the middle of the twentieth century. One hundred years ago, only about 2 percent of those entering public elementary school could expect to graduate from high school. I was told by an urban high school math teacher recently that students in seventh grade in the 1930s learned higher-order math than high school students today. His proof was an ancient seventh-grade math text. What this teacher did not realize is that perhaps only 5 percent of the general population actually was expected to use this text. It would be logical to assume a much higher percentage of students learn the contents of this text by the time they complete high school than learned it in the 1930s.

In my local newspaper recently, an editorial cartoon showed a man and young boy in front of a large map of the United States. The man asked the boy what the map was of, to which the boy replied, "Iraq, of course." This was just another example of our chiding K–12 students about their lack of knowledge, in this case, of geography. I would like to examine this "ignorance" of geography for a moment. Why, for instance, is it important to know all the states and the state capitals? I learned them all and the reader probably did also, by singing a song listing all the capitals in alphabetical order. Of what use has this knowledge been? Nothing against North Dakota, but who really needs to know its capital unless one lives in the state? I happen to have a love for maps and have studied them on my own since I was about seven. I would say that I have developed a thirst for knowledge about these places in the atlas, and also a desire to travel there. I learned geography through my own interest and it was, therefore, important in my intellectual development. The fact that I know the fifty state capitals is irrelevant to my life; however, the deeper understanding of geography learned on my own because of my self-motivation is indeed relevant to my life and my development as a person. Certain aspects of geography are important to be known and appreciated by our children, but they will not be important to them if we present geography as utter regurgitation of facts. The bulimic learning model was how geography was presented to me in school. Unlike mind-numbingly mundane fact memorization of the state capitals, it is imperative to gain an in-depth understanding of other people and other nation-states in order to become better global citizens. So why do our children not care enough about geography and who lives in these places they see on the various maps? It is in a large part because of our schooling model based on the industrial age where all learning has to be measurable, causing us to rely on inane teaching practices. I will contend, however, that in the case of geography, globalization and our American ethnocentricity keep our students from being motivated to gain deep understandings of the world around them.

Globalization, especially the sharing of culture through media, has caused a U.S.-inspired monoculture of consumerism to develop throughout much of the world (Castells 2000). This is one of the criticisms we get from the Muslim world. We change the values of the world either intentionally or unintentionally. And it is not the proliferation and spreading of our most desired values—freedom, (real) democracy, and the pursuit of happiness. These indeed are worthy of disseminating worldwide; rampant consumerism that is void of social responsibility and rife with personal pleasure is not.

Ethnocentricity keeps us from understanding that we could be polluting the values of the rest of the world, as well as those in our own culture. Conservatives fear that our students are becoming less patriotic, which might have something to do with the decrease in trust for authority, a trend that could be traced back to the Vietnam fiasco or perhaps to the realization of de jure and de facto racism. Adults fear that our children are becoming more and more wrapped up in themselves and what happens in their own individual "worlds." The media manipulate our children's minds, telling them to consume based on their own desires, media that are supported by corporatists who, in turn, wield the greatest power over our politicians. Who is to blame for this lack of patriotism and selfishness? Our way of life needs to be examined by each of us and especially by those who are in power. Utilizing a global-age model of schooling can help in this examination and can provide a catalyst for change based on critical pedagogy and democratic learning environments.

SHIFTING, PRAGMATIC KNOWLEDGE

In previous chapters, I have provided the reader with examples of knowledge and qualities that are worthwhile for global age citizens. I have also described the lack of those qualities in the schools and, I hope, have provided the reader with reasons for that lack. I want to give some examples of some specific knowledge or skills that we take for granted in the schools that may or may not be worthwhile in the global age. The two that irk me the most are math calculation and spelling skills. There might be a deemphasis on these skills in the schools that would be attributed to technology; math calculations are made quickly and easily on electronic calculators and spelling deficiencies are overcome by spell-check devices on word processing software. Yet, all too often I read in a letter to the editor that "kids today can't spell" or "kids don't know their times tables." These letters, embarrassingly often, are written by educators. So what? How will these skills help them thrive in the global village? I recall staying up late at night working on my times tables so that, through memorization, I could quickly recall what 11×11 equals. To this day, I have difficulty remembering this calculation, but I surely memorized it long enough to receive high marks in second or third grade, whenever it was demanded that I regurgitate the answer for a grade.

When confronted with a simple multiplication calculation, I either "guesstimate" or use a calculator. As a language arts teacher, I stopped giving my students spelling words and spelling tests because these tests were merely evaluations of their memorization abilities, rather than their ability to use the language. Instead, I exposed them to some spelling rules (to which there are always exceptions!) in addition to reading lists of words that are often misspelled. And I gave them lists of words that are often not caught by spell-checking software. So spelling, math calculation and, of course, handwriting (who uses longhand anymore?) are not of great need in our schools. If we think about it, we can find many other areas that we no longer need to use our schools' and students' resources to teach. My point is that instead of merely adding "necessary" knowledge onto already overloaded curricula, we should eliminate the irrelevant and useless knowledge that is required of students in our schools. This will make way for learning that is pragmatic and essential in the global age, although it will be a bit discomforting for those who seek refuge from the turbulent world in the sureties of schooling being just like we remembered it.

If one were to read the various state standards, there really is not much that can be argued against as far as importance, and most states are working diligently to align these standards with the mandated tests. Unfortunately, it is how these items are learned that is the problem. By making the curricula a "mile wide and an inch deep," real understanding of content is denied. A deeper understanding of content, as I gained from my self-learning of geography, is of more benefit to students than "covering" it. By using such strategies as thematic learning where students explore a topic thoroughly, examining every aspect of it and the environment in which it exists, students can "cover" the content while also gaining an understanding of it. This type of learning will actually be remembered and, therefore, can be used later in life, in contrast to bulimic learning that is forgotten after it is regurgitated onto the test—but is easily assessed. Easy assessment makes for excellent weapons by those who would destroy public education. It will be quite a struggle to change how we conduct schooling.

PROMOTING AND FACILITATING CHANGE

What I advocate in this book is change. I just gave the reader some examples of how we can change curricula so that they are more relevant to the third wave of civilization. More important is the need for change in how schools and school systems are structured; including a change in *what* students learn (the various curricula) and a change in *how* students learn (a change in instructional methods). This is quite a challenge considering that people generally are uncomfortable with change. The status quo is soothing for most of us. Yet, an old adage first attributed to biologists and now used by organizational theorists is "What stops growing, starts dying." That which strives to keep the status quo cannot survive.

This is best exemplified by the tri-partite theory of institutional change and succession as developed by Arthur Shapiro, William Benjamin, and Jack Hunt (1995). An organization is developed by a charismatic leader who invigorates the environment, including the people in the organization. This leader eventually loses interest or simply tires of his or her role and leaves the organization behind. Leadership is then taken over by a "planner" who may have worked with the charismatic leader to help that person organize his or her thoughts and actions. The planner, without another charismatic leader, is unable to sustain the excitement of the initial start-up of the organization. The organization becomes bureaucratic in nature, striving to keep things just the way they are, and is "led" by bureaucrats. Of course, this organization will die because it does not change to meet the needs of the ever-changing environment around it (marketplace and customers). It takes another charismatic leader to step in to save the organization, to revitalize it. The cycle then starts over again, unless the organization is allowed to die before the arrival of another charismatic leader. The tri-partite theory advocates a leader who acts as a synergist and who has the qualities of both the charismatic leader and the planner—the ability to inspire and plan for change, thus ensuring the perpetual life of the organization.

The life of the tri-partite cycle varies according to the organization's environment. Most businesses cannot function for long in the bureaucratic stage because the marketplace (competition, government regulations) changes almost as rapidly as do the needs and desires of the customer. Large American companies that reaped the benefits of little or no global competition following World War II found that they did not have to change and could exist in the bureaucratic stage until overseas competition arrived. Schools and most government entities have had no pressing catalysts for change. Some competition comes through private schools but, historically, only a small percentage of parents could afford or wanted to make the financial commitment to place their children in such schools. As far back as the 1950s, Paul Mort and William Vincent (1954) argued that schools were twenty-five years behind the best organizational practices of the time. What is frightening is that little has changed in a school's function since then, so one could argue that schools are now seventy-five years behind.

Some predict that vouchers (using tax dollars to allow students to attend private schools) will be a catalyst for change. Unfortunately, this idea is based on the assumption that private schools are somehow superior to public schools. As mentioned previously, controlling the variable of socioeconomic status, private schools are simply no better than public schools. Charter schools are another strategy used by politicians to spur schools to change. They erroneously believe that change will occur by relieving schools of most of the burden of government regulations, of bureaucracy. Charter schools, unfortunately, not only skim from the other public schools their most successful students but, I have no doubt, will quickly move into the bureaucratic stage of the tri-partite cycle. It was most likely a charismatic leader who brought forward the charter, and charismatic leaders tend not to stay in one place for long. A charismatic leader would most likely be an "SP" temperament in the Myers-Briggs Type Indicator. Unfortunately for schools, the SP is not likely to be interested in working in education, especially not for the long haul (Keirsey and Bates 1984).

How do we change schools and schooling? The first criterion for change is to recognize that change is needed. I have spent much of this book arguing for the need for change in schools and schooling. Hopefully, it was fruitful.

The comprehension of what the new global age will require of workers and citizens and comparing this to what is now occurring in the schools should demonstrate to even a hardened critic that change is necessary. Globalization has an effect on economies and cultures; contrast this to the bureaucratic structures and status quo mind-sets of and in education as well as the reactionary forces that would "change" schooling. Ignoring these needs will be catastrophic to our economy, our nation, and our society. That which does not change, dies.

Those who would change schools must be trusted by those who are the stakeholders of public education: businesses, communities, parents, teachers, and students. And, hopefully, many stakeholders are actually involved in the designing and implementation of this change. School change agents must be able to support the necessity of change in regard to its value for the stakeholders, especially our children. School change is not to promote one's career, or one's social or political ideologies. A change agent can be charismatic, as described in tri-partite theory, but change instigated by a charismatic leader will last only as long as he or she remains in the organization, which would not be long. The synergistic leader, on the other hand, may be able to "share" a vision, as Peter Senge advocates (1990). This sharing would ensure trust among the stakeholders; if they hold the same beliefs about the organization's future as does the leader, then it is not simply the leader they are following, but their own values.

Another way to ensure that proposed change is trusted by the stakeholders is to have change come from the grassroots or "bottom up." Parents, teachers, or even students (but not likely, given this latter group's lack of power) can instigate change. As they constitute the majority of the stakeholders directly affected by schooling, trust should be a certainty. Change can occur if enough of those in power or who would be in power gain the trust of the stakeholders and then formulate a vision for their organization and for schooling that is congruent with the needs of the global age. Those in power must then share this vision with the majority who are not. This places a great amount of the responsibility on those who are paid to take on the most responsibility. Management lacking responsibility to initiate effective change caused U.S. industry to belatedly embrace quality management and remain the dominant player in the world economy.

At this point, I wish to recall the lessons we learned from W. Edwards Deming who sought to ensure that organizations continuously strive toward quality of service and product. Deming found through his work with the Japanese, and then later in America, that the problem in an organization's failure did not lie with the worker, but with management and their ineffective (if not harmful) strategies. The current attack on teachers and labeling those teachers as incompetents could be missing the point, according to quality theory. How has school management changed to meet the new needs of the stakeholders, needs that are a result of our schools moving into the global age? The answer is, it has not. Schools are structured and operated in essentially the same manner as they were a century ago, that is, as bureaucracies. As described earlier, a flatter, more responsive organization with Theory Y leadership sharing power is crucial for this new age. Students cannot be expected to thrive in these work environments if they have not experienced them.

For the past two decades, school boards, then gradually state governments, and now the federal government, have believed the problem with low student achievement (perceived or real) was the result of unprepared teachers. The blame is tossed back and forth between teachers' unions and colleges of education. Many of those currently in power seek to teacher-proof the curriculum (the standards movement) and resurrect the old "normal school" model of preparing teachers—that is, give them two years of technical training at a community college instead of a university education. They can continue to learn on the job through teacher workshops provided by the districts and the states. This would support the argument that teaching is merely a technical science that anyone can learn and do. Teacher-proof curricula and lock-step curricular programs would ensure that every student learns the same thing at the same time. This, of course, is contrary to sound learning theory, but try explaining this to politicians who, while shirking their responsibilities of ensuring social justice for all and placing these responsibilities on the shoulders of the lowly paid and powerless teacher, are trying to appear as the get-tough American hero to their constituents. Moreover, by de-professionalizing teaching, politicians would be able to pay them even less, leaving more money to be spent on the "back end" of society: the military-police-prison-security industrial complex.

Although Deming was a statistician, he soon found that constant testing of product and service did not lead to better quality (1986). Instead, he designed a quality process that ensured quality the first time (no need for remediation) by using intrinsic motivators. For too long, American managers have relied on the extrinsic motivators of salary and benefits, and the demotivator of punishment. Deming had the Japanese desiring to go to work by making work a fun and exciting place to be, by fostering a team spirit throughout the organization. Schools can foster this same spirit through the use of learning communities and by revolting against the testing movement, which is exactly what Deming had found to be ineffective in raising quality. It is ironic that as the quality movement has flourished in U.S. industry, the schools have been forced into practices that are the antithesis of quality. What is being advocated currently is not good business practice but poor, ineffective, and damaging practices left over from the industrial age.

Another aspect of Deming's quality movement is the desire to have those "in the trenches" become problem solvers, problem solving being a by-product of critical thinking, which factory-model schooling does not promote (1986). Senge's learning organization stresses the importance that everyone in an organization be able to resolve conflict in product and process as well as in relations among workers (1990). Our children do not resolve problems among themselves in schools because our incessant supervision does not allow for this. They do not solve complex academic problems in the classroom as this is not easily assessed on a pencil-and-paper test and, therefore, cannot be held against them and their school in this era of accountability. (A colleague of mine uses an analogy to describe the lack of "logical" validity of standardized testing and other weapons used in the accountability movement. He says that as a husband he cannot be tested as good or bad on a paper-and-pencil test. Nor can he be assessed by examining his actions on one particular day. The whole of his marriage must be examined in order to assess his worth as a husband; a one-test-per-year method would be unfair and invalid. The same is true for our children and their learning in that their whole experience must be assessed. Standardized testing can only be used as a tool for teachers to help them understand a child's learning or ability to learn. Using it as a political weapon is indeed invalid.)

The old merit pay debate is being dusted off by states and school districts around the nation. I am a firm believer that a person should be paid what he or she is worth, but I have yet to see a teacher assessment instrument that accurately measures a constructivist teacher. Furthermore, Deming believed that performance ratings only spawned competition, not cooperation (1986). It is through cooperation, he contended, that quality can thrive. No one goes into teaching for the monetary compensation; therefore, using promises of increased salaries to motivate teachers is fruitless. Instead, those who control schooling should work to increase teacher quality through the development of global school organizations. With increased public confidence in schools and the shattering of the culture of distrust will come higher pay for the entire teaching profession.

Increasing quality in an organization, in both its products and services, requires a focus on the main point of the quality movement: focusing on the needs of the customer. Deming sought customer approval and data relating to their desires as ways to mold companies. "Mold" is not the correct term with respect to organizations, and Deming would agree, because it connotes rigidity. Global organizations need to be ready to change at a moment's notice because the environment is forever changing. Schools are notoriously rigid due to their bureaucratic structures and the management styles employed in them. This rigidity can be rectified by acknowledging the need for change to meet the needs of the global age, by instituting flexible (or fluid), flatter structures, and by quality management principles.

Finally, change takes time. The Japanese seek "kaizen" in their organizations, a term that means "continuous improvement." Change in organizations is slow and is even slower, if even existent, in schools. Change will come quickly to an organization that depends on profits to keep it open. Schools do not depend on profit, at least not public schools. They stay open as long as taxpayers believe that they are performing. The media rightfully have pointed out that schools are not performing, but the reason for this nonperformance is misunderstood. Instead of looking ahead at what the global age requires of its workers and citizens, those who control schools fondly look backward to a time that denied the development of students into global workers and citizens. The standards movement spawned by the accountability movement endeavors to take schooling backward, further and further away from the third wave in which we currently find ourselves. The results will be devastating for our schools, our children, and our society unless, somehow, forward-thinking individuals can wrest control from the those who control our schools and a global-age schooling model can be instituted.

NINE

Our Moral Obligation

I fervently believe it is our moral obligation to prepare all our children to succeed in the global age. Different sets of traits, skills, and knowledge are required of workers in the global economy, and these are not being fostered in our schools. Sweden's population is 15 percent immigrants, many coming from Third World nations (in the school district I last studied, some schools had as many as 85 percent of their students either born in other countries or their parents were). The Swedes, by promoting such social values as tolerance and equity, appear to be establishing themselves as a model for globalized nations. Scholars contend that democracy will continue to flourish in the third wave of civilization. If this form of democracy is to be an empowering public democracy instead of a private, limited participant democracy as we now condone, then it is crucial that our citizens receive an education that is pertinent to the global age as well as have the requisite knowledge and desire to be politically active. Advocating industrial-age skills such as obedience to authority does not prepare students for perpetuating a true democracy or, for that matter, to thrive in any global organization.

SOCIAL JUSTICE AND DEMOCRACY

When I suggest that it is our moral obligation to ensure that all are prepared for the new wave of civilization, I include those who are less fortunate, in our own nation as well as in others. If all races and social classes in the United States continue to be denied equitable opportunities to participate in the global age, our society might very well implode. Paulo Freire (1970) advocated critical pedagogy to educate the underclasses in order to empower themselves. This empowerment establishes the public democracy advocated by David Sehr (1997) where all people are capable and willing to have their voices heard and acted upon by those in power so that they can and will share power. Establishing critical pedagogy in a society as class-conscious as ours is an unlikely if not dangerous goal due to the unwillingness of those who hold power to share this with others. I support Freire, Sehr, and Henry Giroux (1989; 2003) in their attempts to empower those who have for so long been disempowered, and I believe the only effective means to this end is to "level the playing field" by establishing equitable education systems in the United States—education systems that actually meet the needs of society's neediest, not simply preparing them to be obedient or unemployed service workers.

Moreover, as the one remaining world superpower, we cannot shirk our responsibility to the rest of humanity; therefore, we must become active participants in international educational organizations such as UNESCO—not dictators of policy as we desire to be in the United Nations and North Atlantic Treaty Organization. With our nation's position of military strength and our relative prosperity, we would still do well to remember the Swedish moral that no one blade of grass should stick out. Those fortunate few who have found great wealth in our nation would also be wise to not be that blade rising above the others. Whether it is our country or the opulent wealthy within our society, the tallest blade of grass is the first target for those who are less powerful. Despite our desire to wear a white hat and ride into town as the cowboy hero, bringing with us all the "goodness" of a market society and (limited) democracy, our presence and values are not desired by many in the world nor should they unquestioningly be so. We have plenty to fix in our own house before we can even attempt to be role models for the rest of the world, especially where education is concerned.

I acknowledge it would be frightening for most of us who live relatively comfortable lives to think that we may have to contribute a little more so that others can enjoy the benefits of the global age, which is a necessity to create equity. But more frightening would be a world with impenetrable barriers between the haves and have-nots, barriers built to insulate the well-to-do from the ugliness that is poverty. A literature professor in my undergraduate studies once said that we Americans "anesthetize ourselves with aesthetics." We consume and live the American dream of opulent material wealth so that we do not have to face that which is gruesome. The wealthy fear a redistribution of wealth, and they should—they have the most to lose. A redistribution of wealth is a real probability if we were to actually follow through and educate all children for the global age. Real education brings with it power. And not the type of education that is measured on pencil-and-paper tests, the type used in high-stakes testing by state governments in order to control schools. Education, as defined by UNESCO, Freire, Sehr, and Giroux, among others who know the true meaning of democracy, empowers all who partake in its processes. It is this "deep-understanding-with-a-follow-through-commitment" type of education that I have tried to describe and advocate to the reader.

Despite my criticisms of our political system, I do not promote one major political party over the other because neither has an understanding of what our citizens and workers should know, do, and be like in the global age. In the 2000 presidential race, I was disheartened not to hear a forward-thinking education plan described by either Senator Gore or Governor Bush. Both the Republican and Democratic education policies involved more of the same: testing, testing, and if that does not work, more testing; testing of students, teachers, and anybody else that might pass through a school. Both candidates were reacting to the culture of distrust that they and other politicians use to mask the failings of their own social policies, policies that have deepened and widened the chasm between the haves and the have-nots.

I cannot praise the work of my colleagues in universities either, especially those of us in colleges of education. We have not been able to promote the changes necessary in schools so that they could evolve into third-wave preparatory institutions. This inability emanates from a lack of foresight, insight, and willingness to leave the "ivory tower" in order to go out to the schools and build trusting relationships, although great headway is being made with the advent of the professional development school, a model far too scarce on the educational landscape. The public does not trust K–12 education; that is clear. Yet, the level of distrust that the public, especially politicians, has for colleges of education is at a dangerous level. Politicians say it is the colleges of education's fault that we have poor quality teaching in public schools, and to a point, they are correct.

Although I would contend colleges of education have exposed preservice teachers to correct theory, we were and are, however, unable to connect that theory to the reality that is found in the schools, except in isolated incidences (such as some professional development schools). Worse, we failed to produce change agents in schools that could alter the reality that is the school, a reality that mirrors the industrial age. Colleges of education desperately need to promote their theories through better public relations and connections to all the public, especially schools, parents, and politicians. Otherwise, colleges of education will no longer be deemed necessary by the public and especially by politicians. I would say that many people already consider them worthless. Universities are and have been on track in their theories; they simply have not been able to incite their graduates to actualize these theories both at the classroom level and at the highest levels of administration.

As noted in the previous chapters, there has been some recent conjecture that teacher training return to the "normal school" model, where teachers are given a technical training in a community college or through district professional development. These newly minted teachers would then be allowed to mature under the guidance of the school district, which would ensure that they became just like the other teachers. The danger of this model is, obviously, that teachers would not be professionals (if they actually are, anyway, due to their lack of autonomy) and would simply be lowly paid technicians (instead of lowly paid professionals). What is truly frightening is the result of this model: absolutely no change toward effective schooling, that is, schooling that fosters learning for the global age. No change in schools or a return to yesteryear does, however, result in change of sorts: a deepening and widening of the chasm between the rich and poor in this nation that will find more security measures needed to ward off the poor. Despite the burgeoning military-police-prison-security industrial complex, we may yet experience a backlash by the underprivileged populations that would result in a permanent scarring of our national culture.

Increased security and backlash of the disempowered are unnecessary if we can ensure that all children in all schools are prepared to meet the new challenges of the global age. This will require new curricula, new instructional methods, new roles for both teachers and students, and new school structures. These changes are impossible without the understanding of educators, the general public, the business community, and our politicians of what is needed to succeed in the third wave of civilization. A new way of thinking about schooling is required—a "metanoia" according to Peter Senge (1990), or to use a worn-out expression, a paradigm shift. With this metanoia comes the commitment to alter a system of schools designed for the industrial age to one that is fluid enough to meet the needs of the ever-changing new age, an age that requires more than military or even economic might. A nation will thrive in the global age only with empowered, socially mature citizens to promote and nurture the proliferation of real democracy—a democracy that itself requires continuous change.

Appendix A

Swedish National Curriculum for The Compulsory School, The Pre-School Class, and The Leisure-Time Centre (LPO 94)

FUNDAMENTAL VALUES

Democracy forms the basis of the national school system. The Education Act (1985: 1100) stipulates that all school activity should be carried out in accordance with fundamental democratic values and that each and everyone working in the school should encourage respect for the intrinsic value of each person as well as for the environment we all share (Chapter 1, §2).

The school has the important task of imparting, instilling and forming in pupils those fundamental values on which our society is based.

The inviolability of human life, individual freedom and integrity, the equal value of all people, equality between women and men and solidarity with the weak and vulnerable are all values that the school should represent and impart. In accordance with the ethics borne by Christian tradition and Western humanism, this is achieved by fostering in the individual a sense of justice, generosity of spirit, tolerance and responsibility.

Education in the school shall be non-denominational.

The task of the school is to encourage all pupils to discover their own uniqueness as individuals and thereby actively participate in social life by giving of their best in responsible freedom.

UNDERSTANDING AND
COMPASSION FOR OTHERS

Concern for the welfare and development of the individual should characterise all school activity. It should also actively resist any tendency towards bullying or persecution. Xenophobia and intolerance must be actively confronted with knowledge, open discussion and effective measures.

The internationalisation of Swedish society and increasing cross-border mobility place great demands on people's ability to live together and appreciate the values that are to be found in cultural diversity. Awareness of one's own cultural origins and sharing a common cultural heritage provides a secure identity which it is important to develop, together with the ability to empathise with the values and conditions of others. The school is a social and cultural meeting place with both the opportunity and the responsibility to foster this ability among all who work there.

OBJECTIVITY AND OPEN APPROACHES

As well as being open to different ideas and encouraging their expression, the school should also emphasise the importance of forming personal standpoints and provide pupils with opportunities for doing this. Education should be objective and encompass a range of different approaches so that all parents will feel able to send their children to school confident that they will not be prejudiced in favour of a particular view.

All who work in the school should uphold the fundamental values that are stated in the Education Act and in this curriculum, and should very clearly disassociate themselves from anything that conflicts with these values.

AN EQUIVALENT EDUCATION

Education should be adapted to each pupil's circumstances and needs. Based on the pupils' background, earlier experiences, language, and knowledge, it should promote the pupils' further learning and acquisition of knowledge.

The Education Act stipulates that the education provided within each type of school should be of equivalent value, irrespective of where in the country it is provided (Chapter 1, §2).

National goals specify the norms for equivalence. However, equivalent education does not mean that the education should be the same everywhere or that the resources of the school shall be allocated equally. Account should also be taken of the varying circumstances and needs of pupils as well as the fact that there are a variety of ways of attaining these goals. Furthermore, the school has a special responsibility for those pupils who for, different reasons experience difficulties in attaining the goals that have been set for the education.

For this reason, education can never be the same for all. The school should actively and consciously further equal rights and opportunities for men and women. The way in which girls and boys are treated and assessed in school as well as the demands and expectations that are placed on them, contributes to their perception of gender differences. The school has a responsibility to counteract traditional gender roles and should therefore provide pupils with the opportunity of developing their own abilities and interests irrespective of their sexual identity.

RIGHTS AND OBLIGATIONS

The school should make clear to pupils and parents the goals of the education, the requirements of the school and the rights and obligations of pupils and guardians. A basic precondition for pupils and guardians to exercise influence is that the individual school clearly sets out its goals, its content and its working structures. This is important not least as a basis for individual choice at school.

It is not in itself sufficient that education imparts knowledge of fundamental democratic values. It must also be carried out using democratic working methods and prepare pupils for active participation in civic life. By participating in the planning and evaluation of their daily education, and exercising choices over courses, subjects, themes and activities, pu-

pils will develop their ability to exercise influence and take responsibility.

THE TASK OF THE SCHOOL

The task of the school is to promote learning by stimulating the individual into acquiring knowledge. In partnership with the home the school
should promote the development of pupils into responsible persons and
members of society (Chapter 1, article 2). The school-should be perme-
ated by concern for the individual, consideration and generosity. In a
deeper sense education and upbringing involve developing and passing
on our cultural heritage—values, traditions, language, knowledge—
from one generation to the next. The school should support families in
their responsibility for the children's upbringing and development. As a
result there must be close co-operation between the school and home.
Creative activities and play are essential components of active learning.

The school has the task of imparting fundamental values and promoting pupils' learning in order to prepare them to live and work in society.
It should therefore impart the more unvarying forms of knowledge that
constitute the common frame of reference that all in society need. Pupils should be able to keep their bearings in a complex reality where
there is a vast flow of information and where the rate of change is rapid.
This is why methods of acquiring and using new knowledge and skills
are important. It is also necessary for pupils to develop their ability to
critically examine facts and relationships and appreciate the consequences of the various alternatives facing them. Language, learning, and
the development of a personal identity are all closely related. By providing a wealth of opportunities for discussion, reading and writing, all pupils should be able to develop their ability to communicate and thus
enhance confidence in their own language abilities.

An important task for the school is to provide a general but coherent
view. It should also provide pupils with opportunities for taking initiatives and responsibility as well as creating the preconditions for developing their ability to work independently and solve problems. Particularly
in the early years of schooling, play is very important in helping pupils
to acquire knowledge.

It is important that education provides general perspectives. An historical perspective enables pupils to prepare for the future and develop their ability to think in dynamic terms. An environmental perspective provides them with opportunities not only to take responsibility for the environment in areas where they themselves can have a direct influence, but also to form a personal position with respect to global environmental issues. Teaching should illuminate how the functions of society and how our ways of living and working can best be adapted to create conditions for sustainable development.

Appendix B

Swedish National Curriculum for the Pre-School

ABOUT THE CURRICULUM
FOR THE PRE-SCHOOL

This is the first curriculum for the pre-school, which means that the pre-school will now constitute the first step in the education system for children and young persons. Since January 1st 1998, the National Agency for Education has acted as the supervisory authority for the pre-school as well as for other pre-school activities and school-age child care. The legislation was incorporated into the Education Act on the same date.

The curriculum is based on a division of responsibility where the state determines the overall goals and guidelines for the pre-school and where the municipalities take responsibility for implementation. In its structure the curriculum of the preschool is consistent with the other curricula for the school system. As a result of the introduction of a curriculum for the pre-school, the education system as a whole now comprises three curricula, one for the pre-school (Lpfö 98), a second for the compulsory school system also covering the pre-school class and the leisure-time centres (Lpo 94) as well as a curriculum for the upper secondary school system (Lpf 94). The aim is that the three curricula should link into each other and take a common view of knowledge, development and learning.

THE CURRICULUM APPLIES
TO THE PRE-SCHOOL

This curriculum applies to the pre-school, i.e., the pedagogical activities for children in the pre-schools for which the municipalities are responsible. The curriculum will also provide a foundation for assessing quality requirements when determining whether an individual preschool fulfils the stipulated requirements. The curriculum will also be applicable to family day-care homes.

The curriculum for the pre-school replaces the pedagogical programme and the guidelines issued by the National Board of Health and Welfare, which were used earlier to steer these activities. The curriculum is an ordinance with binding provisions issued by the Government. The curriculum will steer the pre-school and contains the requirements the state imposes on the pre-school. It also expresses the requirements and expectations children and parents may make on the pre-school.

The curriculum sets out the fundamental values for the pre-school, the tasks, goals and guidelines for pre-school activities. However, the curriculum does not lay down the means by which goals shall be attained. This is an issue primarily for the staff working in the pre-school. The principal organizer is responsible for ensuring that the pre-school is in a position to attain the goals of the curriculum. The development and learning of the individual child will be supported in close co-operation between pre-school and home.

THE STRUCTURE OF THE CURRICULUM

The introductory section of the curriculum deals with the fundamental values and tasks of the pre-school. The goals and guidelines that follow thereafter are to be understood against this background.

Goals and guidelines for the pre-school are given for the following areas:

- Norms and values
- Development and learning
- Influence of the child
- Pre-school and home
- Co-operation between the pre-school class, the school and the leisure-time center

The goals set out directions for the work of the pre-school and contain targets for quality development in the pre-school. The goals in the pre-school curriculum are set up as goals to be aimed at. They stipulate what the preschool should aim at in terms of the individual development and learning of the child. Continuity between the curricula will be easier to establish as a result of setting up common goals for both the preschool and school.

In the pre-school the outcome of the individual child will not be formally assessed in terms of grades and evaluation. The pre-school provides pedagogical activity which children can begin and participate in at different ages over varying periods of time. The pre-school should be secure, developmental and rich in learning opportunities for all children participating on the basis of each child's individual conditions.

The guidelines in the curriculum stipulate that the goal-oriented work of the preschool will apply to the work team itself and all those who work in the pre-school. The work team refers to the staff who have the pedagogical responsibility for a particular group of children.

PLANNING, IMPLEMENTATION, ASSESSMENT AND DEVELOPMENT

The activities of the pre-school should be planned, implemented, assessed and developed in relation to the goals set up in the curriculum. It is important that the methods of assessment developed are clearly related to the goals set up for the activities and that they contribute to the overall development of the pedagogical work. By documenting pedagogical activity, activities in the pre-school can be made more explicit and thus provide an important basis for discussion and assessment of the quality of activities and the need for development.

Attaining the goals of the curriculum requires well-educated staff, who are provided with the opportunity to enhance their competence and receive the support necessary for them to carry out their tasks in a professional manner. Fulfilling the tasks of the pre-school also imposes high demands on leadership. The municipalities in their capacity as principal organisers are responsible for this.

THE CURRICULUM IS BASED ON THE EDUCATION ACT

Chapter 2a, paragraphs 1–12 in the Education Act (1985:1100) contain the basic provisions on how pre-school activities are to be organised.

The Act stipulates that the municipalities are obliged to provide pre-school activity of high quality without unreasonable delay. This obligation concerns all children whose parents are working or studying, or who need child care support as well as for all children in need of special support. The task of the preschool is to organise and run pedagogical activities. There should be staff with the requisite education or experience capable of satisfying the child's need for care and good pedagogical activities. The size and composition of the child groups should be appropriate. The premises should be suitable for their purpose. Activities should be based on the individual needs of each child. Children who need special support for their development should receive care related to their needs.

REFERENCES

Apple, M. W. 2000. Between neoliberalism and neoconservatism: Education and conservatism in a global context. In *Globalization and education: Critical perspectives*, edited by N. C. Burbules and C. A. Torres. New York: Routlege.

―――. 2001. *Educating the "right" way: Markets, standards, God, and inequality.* New York: RoutledgeFalmer.

Applefield, J. M., R. Huber, and M. Moallem. 2000. Constructivism in theory and practice: Toward a better understanding. *High School Journal* 84, no. 2: 35–53.

Aronowitz, S., and H. A. Giroux. 1991. *Postmodern education: Politics, culture, and social criticism.* Minneapolis: University of Minnesota Press.

Atwell, N. 1987. *In the middle: Writing, reading, and learning with adolescents.* Upper Montclair, N.J.: Boynton/Cook.

Bloom, B. 1956. *The classification of educational goals.* New York: Longman.

Castells, M. 2000. *End of millennium*, 2nd ed. Malden, Mass.: Blackwell.

Cotton, K. 1996. *School size, school climate, and student performance: Close-up #20.* Portland, Oreg.: Northwest Regional Educational Laboratory.

Delors, J., ed. 1998. Education for the twenty-first century: Issues and prospects. Paris, France: UNESCO.

Delpit, L. 1995. *Other people's children: Cultural conflict in the classroom.* New York: New Press.

Deming, W. E. 1986. *Out of the crisis.* Cambridge, Mass.: Massachusetts Institute of Technology.

Erikson, R. J. 2000. Compulsory education in Sweden. *Education* 120, 3.

Freire, P. 1970. *Pedagogy of the oppressed.* Translated by M. B. Ramos. New York: Seabury.

―――. 1973. *Education for critical consciousness.* New York: Seabury.

Gardner, H. 1999. *The disciplined mind: What all students should understand.* New York: Simon and Schuster.

Giroux, H. A. 2003. *The abandoned generation: Democracy beyond the culture of fear.* New York: Palgrave MacMillan.

Giroux, H. A., and P. L. McLaren, eds. 1989. *Critical pedagogy, the state, and cultural struggle.* Albany: State University of New York Press.

Greenberg, D. 1992. *The Sudbury Valley School experience,* 3rd ed. Framington, Mass.: Sudbury Valley School Press.

Handy, C. 1994. *The age of paradox.* Boston, Mass.: Harvard Business School Press.

Howard, B. C., S. McGee, and N. Schwartz. 2000. The experience of constructivism: Transforming teacher epistemology. *Journal of Research on Computing in Education* 32, no. 4: 455–65.

Ingersoll, R. M. 2001. Teacher turnover and teacher shortages: An organizational analysis. *American Educational Research Journal* 38: 499–534.

———. 2002. The teacher shortage: A case of wrong diagnosis and wrong prescription. *NASSP Bulletin* 86: 16–31.

Irvine, J. J. 1991. *Black students and school failure: Policies, practices, and prescriptions.* New York: Praeger.

Johnson, J. O., and M. Gahler. 1997. Family dissolution, family reconstitution, and children's educational careers: Recent evidence for Sweden. *Demography* 34: 277–93.

Keirsey, D., and M. Bates. 1984. *Please understand me: Character and temperament types,* 5th ed. Del Mar, Calif.: Prometheus Nemesis.

Kummerow, J. M., N. J. Barger, and L. K. Kirby. 1997. *WORKTypes.* New York: Warner Books.

Loeffler, M. H. 2002. The essence of Montessori. *Montessori Life* 14, no. 1: 34–36.

MacLeod, J. 1995. *Ain't no makin' it: Aspirations and attainment in a low-income neighborhood.* Boulder, Colo.: Westview Press.

Marlowe, B. A., and M. L. Page. 1998. *Creating and sustaining the constructivist classroom.* Thousand Oaks, Calif.: Corwin Press.

Maslow, A. H. 1987. *Motivation and personality,* 3rd ed. New York: Harper and Row.

McGregor, D. 1960. *The human side of enterprise.* New York: McGraw-Hill.

Mort, P. R., and W. S. Vincent. 1954. *Introduction to American education.* New York: McGraw-Hill.

Myers, I. B., and P. B. Myers. 1995. *Gifts differing: Understanding personality type.* Palo Alto, Calif.: Davies-Black.

National Center for Education Statistics (NCES). 1999. *Highlights of the Third International Mathematics and Science Study TIMSS: Overview and key findings across grade levels.* Washington, D.C.: U.S. Department of Education.

————. 2000. *Indicators of school crime and safety, 2000.* Available at nces.ed-.gov/pubs2001/crime2000

Ogbu, J. U. 2003. *Black American students in an affluent suburb: A study of academic disengagement.* Mahwah, N.J.: Lawrence Erlbaum.

The OJJDP Statistical Briefing Book. 1999. Washington, D.C.: Office of Juvenile Justice and Delinquency Prevention.

Oxley, D. 1994. Organizing schools into small units: Alternatives to homogeneous grouping. *Phi Delta Kappan* 75: 521–26.

Powell, M. 2000. Can Montessorians and constructivists really be friends? *Montessori Life* 12, no. 1: 44–51.

Raywid, M. A. 1998. Small schools: A reform that works synthesis of research. *Educational Leadership* 29: 10–13.

Rose, L. C., and A. M. Gallup. 2002. The 34th annual Phi Delta Kappa/Gallup poll of the public's attitudes toward public schools. *Phi Delta Kappan* 84, no. 2: 41–56.

The Secretary's Commission on Achieving Necessary Skills (SCANS). 1992. *Learning a living: A blueprint for high performance. A SCANS report for America 2000. Part I.* Washington, D.C.: U.S. Department of Labor.

Sehr, D. T. 1997. *Education for public democracy.* Albany: State University of New York Press.

Senge, P. M. 1990. *The fifth discipline: The art and practice of the learning organization.* New York: Doubleday/Currency.

Shapiro, A. S. 2000. *Leadership for constructivist schools.* Lanham, Md.: Scarecrow Press.

Shapiro, A. S., W. F. Benjamin, and J. J. Hunt. 1995. *Curriculum and schooling: A practitioner's guide.* Palm Springs, Calif.: ETC Publications.

Skolverket 2001. The Swedish school system: Child care in Sweden. Available at: www.skolverket.se/english/system/child accessed Swedish Institute 1998. Higher education in Sweden. (Publication No. FS 83 1 Ep.) Stockholm: Swedish Institute.

Toffler, A. 1970. *Future shock.* New York: Random House.

————. 1980. *The third wave.* New York: Morrow.

Weiner, L. 1993. *Preparing teachers for urban schools.* New York: Teachers College Press.

Wilson, B. L., and H. D. Corbett. 2001. *Listening to urban kids: School reform and the teachers they want.* Albany: State University of New York Press.

INDEX

accountability, 1, 2, 27, 29
al Qaeda, 43
Apple, Michael, 21, 34, 35, 47
Atwell, Nancie, 144–145
authentic assessment, 32

Benjamin, William, 180
Bible, 37, 68, 109
Bloom, Benjamin, 41
Boone, Daniel, 76
Bracey, Gerald, 18
Brazil, 106
Brett, George, 71
Briggs, Katherine Cook, 164
Briggs-Myers, Isabel, 164
Broderick, Matthew, 139
Brown v. Topeka Board of Education,
    114
Bush, George W., 31, 35, 77, 78, 98,
    189
Bush, George H. W., 77

Carter, Jimmy, 71, 77
Castells, Manuel, 43
charter schools, 181
China, 15, 84
collaboration, 7, 49, 50, 51, 63, 83, 91,
    120, 146, 147, 151, 158
collectivism, 45, 76, 82, 84, 86, 91, 92
constructivism, 17, 103, 134–135
control in schools, 65, 67–69, 72, 141,
    142, 149, 159, 161, 162; of stu-
    dents, 8, 9, 60–64, 67, 69–72, 111

Deming, W. Edwards, 25, 82–84, 90,
    129, 183–185
democracy, "real" or "true" or "pub-
    lic," 1, 11, 14, 79, 80, 101, 108, 116,
    130, 143, 150, 187; active partici-
    pation in, 1, 107, 123, 171; social
    dimensions of, 15, 70, 72, 93, 95,
    104, 105, 127
Dewey, John, 24, 107, 135
Douglas, Kirk, 77
Dukakis, Michael, 77

Elementary & Secondary Education
    Act of 2001, 8, 28, 30–33, 35, 46,
    97–99, 123, 136, 138, 139, 146,
    152, 153
Enron, 45, 71, 94
ESEA. *See* Elementary & Secondary
    Education Act of 2001

facilitator, teacher as, 12, 59, 120, 137
Florida, schools, 7, 9, 16, 32, 61, 68;
    "A+ plan," 9, 30
Freire, Paulo, 105, 119, 142, 187, 189

Gardner, Howard, 172
Gates Foundation, 136, 152
Germany, 25, 26, 99

207

G.I. Bill, 27, 40
Giroux, Henry, 188, 189
Global Crossing, 45, 71, 94

Handy, Charles, 41
heroism, 77–82, 92
Hunt, Jack, 180

Illinois, 38, 39
Indiana, 38
individualism, 75, 78, 81, 101
Indonesia, 84
Iran-Contra affair, 71
Iowa, 27, 28
Iraq, 71, 177

Japan, 25, 26, 49, 82–84, 99, 110,
    183–185
Jefferson, Thomas, 78
Jim Crow laws, 43, 89
Johnson, Lyndon B., 18

kaizen, 185
Kennedy, John F., 25
Kentucky, 38
King, Martin Luther, Jr., 76
Kurdistan, 15

learning communities, 124, 153,
    157–159
Lincoln, Abraham, 38, 76
Locke, John, 78

MacArthur, Douglas, 25
MacLeod, Jay, 89
Maslow, Abraham, 100
MBTI. *See* Myers-Briggs Type Indi-
    cator
McDonald's, 17, 28, 47
McGregor, Douglas, 162

media, 42, 70, 87, 127, 149, 176, 178,
    185
Mondale, Walter, 77
Montessori, Maria, 172
Montessori schools, 110, 172–174
Mort, Paul, 191
Myers-Briggs Type Indicator, 163–
    169, 181

Nation at Risk, A, 5, 18, 25, 27, 73,
    112, 138, 159, 161
neoconservative(s), 21, 47, 53, 54, 88,
    93
neoliberal(s) 21, 47–48, 53
No Child Left Behind Act. *See* Ele-
    mentary & Secondary Education
    Act of 2001
North Dakota, 177
Norway, 45

Ogbu, John, 89
organized labor, 43, 118, 119

Page, Rod, 107
Piaget, Jean, 135, 172
Plessy v. Ferguson, 114
poverty, 18, 19, 45, 93
Puritan work ethic, 93; background,
    109

Reagan, Ronald, 25, 77, 78
religious fundamentalists, 43, 67
responsibility in schools, 11, 15, 104,
    110, 118, 137, 142, 145, 147–149;
    of citizens in a democracy, 15, 72,
    93, 127; of politicians in a democ-
    racy, 80, 176, 178
Rogers, Will, 21, 27
Ruth, Babe, 71

SCANS Report, 15
Sehr, David, 79, 188, 189
Senge, Peter, 124, 157, 158, 182, 184, 191
SES. *See* socioeconomic status
Shapiro, Arthur, 180
Singapore, 84
Skolverket, 12, 15, 16, 170
socioeconomic status, 6, 29, 53, 114, 127, 152, 159
Somalia, 15
Soviet Union, 3, 24
Sputnik, 24
stakeholders in schools, 3, 4, 107, 113, 114, 121, 122
standardized testing, 1, 30, 41, 115, 149, 159
standards in schools, 12, 17, 27–29, 97, 139, 159, 186
Steinbeck, John, 134
Sweden, school reform, 2, 4, 17, 45, 115, 116, 143, 155, 160; curricula, 12, 42, 59, 75, 97, 137, 142, 143, 146, 148, 156–158, 170, 173; society, 82, 130, 131, 133, 170, 187; values in schools, 11, 13, 67, 109, 118, 123, 128, 136, 144, 147–149
Sudbury Valley Schools, 174

Taiwan, 84
Tampa, Florida, 8, 10, 16
Taxonomy of Learning, 41
Taylor, Frederick, 44, 48, 139
teacher certification, 33
teacher shortages, 119
Theory X and/or Theory Y management, 116, 145, 150, 162, 163, 165, 168, 183
Third International Math & Science Survey, 3, 174

TIMSS. *See* Third International Math and Science Survey
Toffler, Alvin, 3, 5, 18, 23, 37, 40, 42, 43, 113, 158
Total Quality Management, 25, 48, 84–86, 93, 169
TQM. *See* Total Quality Management
tri-partite theory, 180–181
trust as a value, 10, 93, 108, 127, 150–153; in schools, 11, 13, 72, 102, 104, 149
Twain, Mark, 39, 112
Tyco, 45, 71, 94

UNESCO. *See* United Nations Educational, Social, and Cultural Organization
United Nations Education, Social, and Cultural Organization, 99–101, 188, 189
unions. *See* organized labor

Vietnam, 15, 71, 152, 178, 179
Vincent, William, 181
violence in schools, 70, 103
vision for organizations, 6, 52
vouchers, 30, 54

Watergate, 71
Wayne, John, 76, 77
Witherspoon, Reese, 139
workforce skills, 5, 15, 16, 37, 50–53, 91, 99, 112, 178, 179
World War II, 44, 45, 77, 163, 181

Zapatistas, 43
"zero tolerance" policies in schools, 38, 72

About the Author

R. D. Nordgren's interest in education reform emanates from his seemingly irrelevant public school education, which caused him much frustration as a young adult trying to make sense of the world around him. Nearing the age of thirty, he naively decided to act upon his frustrations by becoming a secondary school teacher so that he could "change the world." What he found was an institution that was virtually unchanged from the impractical one he had known as a child, one that had little if any connection to the "real world."

Believing he could make more of a difference if he were in administration, Nordgren worked on a leadership degree at night while teaching middle school language arts during the day. After less than six years in the classroom, Nordgren took an administrative position at a high school but found that, due to bureaucratic constraints, he was even less capable of fostering change than when he was a teacher. He continued his nighttime studies, earning a doctorate with the intent to become a university professor, where he hoped he could finally "make a difference" by influencing the way schooling looks, is conducted, and how people think about it.